Introduction

- The importance of video editing in today's digital world

- Why Adobe Premiere Pro is a leading choice for video editing

Chapter 1: Getting Started with Adobe Premiere Pro

- Understanding the interface: panels, workspaces, and layout

- Importing media files: videos, audio, and images

- Navigating the timeline and basic editing tools

- Creating a new project and setting project settings

Chapter 2: Building a Solid Foundation

- Exploring the different video formats and codecs

- Understanding resolution, frame rates, and aspect ratios

- The role of project presets and sequence settings

- Organizing your media assets using bins and folders

Chapter 3: Essential Editing Techniques

- Cutting and trimming clips in the timeline

- Using the razor tool for precise cuts

- Understanding the basics of transitions and applying them

- Adding and manipulating audio tracks

Chapter 4: Enhancing Your Video with Effects and Transitions

- Working with video and audio effects

- Applying color correction and grading

- Creating dynamic motion with keyframes

- Adding and customizing transitions for seamless cuts

Chapter 5: Advanced Editing Tools and Techniques

- Utilizing the multi-camera editing feature

- Exploring the power of the nested sequences

- Mastering the art of audio editing and mixing

- Creating and animating text and titles

Chapter 6: Working with Audio

- Importing and editing audio tracks

- Applying audio effects and filters

- Adjusting audio levels and creating a balanced mix

- Syncing audio and video for perfect alignment

Chapter 7: Exporting and Sharing Your Work

- Understanding export settings and formats

- Exporting for different platforms: web, social media, and broadcast

- Creating custom export presets for future projects

- Sharing your work directly from Adobe Premiere Pro

Chapter 8: Efficient Workflows and Productivity Tips

- Keyboard shortcuts to speed up your editing process

- Creating and saving custom workspaces

- Utilizing markers and labels for organization

- Collaboration techniques: sharing projects and working in teams

Chapter 9: Troubleshooting and Common Challenges

- Dealing with playback and rendering issues

- Fixing audio and video synchronization problems

- Solving common export errors

- Troubleshooting performance and system compatibility

Chapter 10: Beyond the Basics: Advanced Techniques

- Green screen (chroma key) editing

- Time remapping and speed manipulation

- Advanced color grading and correction

- Creating visual effects using Adobe Premiere Pro

Conclusion

- Reflecting on your journey from novice to Adobe Premiere Pro enthusiast

- Embracing a continuous learning mindset for ongoing improvement

- Encouragement to explore more advanced video editing topics and techniques

Introduction
The importance of video editing in today's digital world

In today's digital world, the importance of video editing cannot be overstated. As our lives become increasingly intertwined with technology and visual content, video has emerged as a dominant and influential medium for communication, entertainment, education, and marketing. Video editing plays a pivotal role in shaping the way we perceive and engage with this dynamic medium.

Visual Dominance and Engagement:
Human beings are inherently visual creatures. We process visual information faster and more effectively than any other form of content. In a world saturated with information, videos provide a highly engaging and memorable way to convey messages. Whether it's a short clip on social media, a documentary, a tutorial, or a promotional video, well-edited videos can captivate audiences, leaving a lasting impact.

Effective Communication:
Video editing enhances communication by allowing creators to craft their messages with precision and intention. By carefully selecting shots, arranging sequences, and incorporating visual effects, editors can guide the viewer's attention and evoke specific emotions. Whether it's a heartwarming story, a persuasive argument, or a call to action, video editing

empowers content creators to tell their stories more powerfully.

Storytelling and Emotion:
At its core, video editing is a form of storytelling. Through the arrangement of shots, pacing, and the incorporation of music and sound effects, editors can create a narrative that resonates with the audience on an emotional level. This emotional connection facilitates better understanding and retention of information. Brands, filmmakers, and educators leverage the art of video editing to invoke empathy, inspire action, and foster a deeper connection with their target audiences.

Entertainment and Engagement:
Entertainment has seen a transformative shift with the rise of digital platforms and streaming services. Video content, from short skits to full-length films, is now more accessible than ever. Video editing enhances the entertainment experience by seamlessly piecing together scenes, creating suspense, and controlling the overall pacing. It's what makes binge-watching a series or getting lost in a captivating movie an immersive experience.

Marketing and Branding:
In the realm of marketing, video editing is a potent tool for building and enhancing brand identity. A well-edited video can communicate a brand's values, products, and services in a succinct and compelling

manner. From product demos and customer testimonials to promotional campaigns and advertisements, video editing allows marketers to create content that resonates with their target audience and drives engagement.

Educational Value:

Video editing has also revolutionized education by making complex concepts more accessible and engaging. Educational videos, tutorials, and online courses leverage the visual and auditory aspects of video to convey information effectively. Dynamic editing techniques, such as animations, graphics, and visual aids, enhance the learning experience and cater to different learning styles.

Conclusion:

In a world where attention spans are fleeting and competition for engagement is fierce, video editing has become an essential tool for effective communication, storytelling, and expression. Whether for personal creative projects, business endeavors, educational pursuits, or entertainment ventures, the art of video editing empowers individuals and organizations to craft compelling narratives that captivate, educate, and inspire audiences around the globe. As technology continues to evolve, video editing will undoubtedly remain a cornerstone of our digital landscape, shaping the way we interact with and understand the world around us.

Why Adobe Premiere Pro is a leading choice for video editing

In the ever-evolving landscape of video editing software, Adobe Premiere Pro stands out as a leading choice, revered by both beginners and professionals alike. With its comprehensive suite of features, powerful tools, and seamless integration with other Adobe Creative Cloud applications, Premiere Pro has solidified its position as a go-to solution for video editing. Let's delve into the reasons behind its prominence and explore what sets it apart in the realm of video post-production.

1. Professional-Grade Editing Capabilities:
Adobe Premiere Pro offers a wide array of professional-grade editing features that cater to a broad spectrum of video editing needs. From basic cutting and trimming to advanced color correction, motion graphics, and audio manipulation, the software encompasses a comprehensive toolkit that empowers editors to bring their creative visions to life. Whether you're editing a short video clip, a documentary, a music video, or a full-length feature film, Premiere Pro provides the tools to execute your project with finesse.

2. User-Friendly Interface:
Despite its advanced capabilities, Premiere Pro manages to maintain a user-friendly interface that is accessible to both beginners and seasoned

professionals. The interface is intuitively designed, with panels and workspaces that can be customized to suit individual preferences. This balance between sophistication and usability makes it an ideal platform for those new to video editing, allowing them to gradually explore and master the software's features.

3. Integration with Adobe Creative Cloud:
One of Premiere Pro's standout advantages is its seamless integration with other Adobe Creative Cloud applications. This ecosystem enables smooth collaboration and a streamlined workflow. Assets created in Photoshop, Illustrator, After Effects, and other Adobe tools can be easily imported and manipulated within Premiere Pro, enhancing the overall editing process. This integration fosters a cohesive creative environment, ensuring a consistent visual style across different elements of a project.

4. Versatile Format Support:
In the contemporary video landscape, editors often deal with a plethora of video formats and resolutions. Premiere Pro rises to the challenge by offering extensive format support, allowing editors to work with a diverse range of footage without the hassle of time-consuming conversions. Whether you're editing footage from DSLRs, professional cameras, smartphones, or even raw formats, Premiere Pro can handle it all.

5. Dynamic Editing and Effects:
Premiere Pro empowers editors with dynamic editing techniques that enhance storytelling and visual impact. Its robust timeline functionality enables precise control over every edit, while the integration of powerful effects and transitions opens the door to creative possibilities. From adding cinematic flair to integrating complex motion graphics, Premiere Pro equips editors with the tools they need to elevate their projects.

6. Advanced Color Correction and Grading:
The software's color correction and grading tools are another reason behind its popularity. Premiere Pro offers a dedicated Lumetri Color panel, allowing editors to manipulate colors, contrast, and saturation with precision. This feature is especially valuable for achieving consistent color grading across shots, giving projects a polished and professional look.

7. Regular Updates and Community Support:
Adobe's commitment to enhancing its software translates into regular updates for Premiere Pro. These updates introduce new features, improvements, and bug fixes, ensuring that editors have access to the latest tools and capabilities. Additionally, the software boasts a vibrant community of users, online tutorials, and forums where users can exchange tips, tricks, and solutions to common challenges.
Conclusion:

Adobe Premiere Pro's position as a leading choice for video editing is a result of its unmatched combination of professional-grade capabilities, user-friendly interface, integration with Adobe Creative Cloud, format versatility, dynamic editing tools, advanced color correction, and ongoing updates. Its appeal to both beginners and professionals, as well as its role within a comprehensive creative ecosystem, cements its status as a cornerstone of the modern video editing landscape. As the field of video editing continues to evolve, Adobe Premiere Pro remains at the forefront, empowering creators to bring their visual stories to life with precision and creativity.

Chapter 1: Getting Started with Adobe Premiere Pro
Understanding the interface: panels, workspaces, and layout

When stepping into the world of video editing, particularly with a powerful tool like Adobe Premiere Pro, understanding the software's interface becomes a crucial first step. The interface of Premiere Pro is designed to provide users with a seamless and intuitive environment for crafting their video projects. In this article, we will delve into the components that make up the interface – panels, workspaces, and layout – and explore how they contribute to a cohesive and efficient editing experience.

Exploring the Panels:
Premiere Pro's interface is composed of various panels, each serving a specific function to aid in the editing process. These panels include the Project panel, Source Monitor, Program Monitor, Timeline, Effects Controls, Audio Mixer, and more. Let's take a closer look at some of these key panels:

1. **Project Panel:** This is where you organize and manage your media assets. You can import videos, audio, images, and other media files, which are then organized into bins for easy access.

2. **Source Monitor:** This panel allows you to preview and mark in and out points for clips before adding them to the timeline. It's a useful space for selecting the best parts of your raw footage.

3. **Program Monitor:** The Program Monitor displays the current state of your timeline sequence. It's where you see the video output as you edit, and you can make real-time adjustments to your edits.

4. **Timeline:** The heart of your editing workspace, the Timeline panel is where you arrange and edit your clips to create your final video. You can trim, cut, add effects, and perform various edits in this panel.

5. **Effects Controls:** This panel provides options to apply and adjust video and audio effects to your clips. You can manipulate parameters like scale, position, opacity, and more.

6. **Audio Mixer:** The Audio Mixer panel lets you adjust audio levels and add audio effects. It's essential for achieving a balanced audio mix in your videos.

Creating Custom Workspaces:

Premiere Pro allows users to create and save custom workspaces tailored to their preferences and editing needs. A workspace is a layout configuration that determines how the various panels are arranged on your screen. Customizing your workspace can significantly enhance your editing efficiency.

For instance, you can create a workspace optimized for video editing by arranging panels like the Timeline, Program Monitor, and Effects Controls prominently. On the other hand, if audio editing is your primary focus, you might prioritize the Audio Mixer and waveform displays. The ability to switch between different workspaces makes it easy to adapt to different editing tasks and workflows.

Layout and UI Customization:

The layout of Adobe Premiere Pro is designed with a focus on flexibility and adaptability. You can arrange panels by dragging and dropping them to different positions, docking them to different sides of the screen, or even creating floating panels for quick access. The software remembers your layout preferences, so you can easily pick up where you left off in your editing process.

Furthermore, Premiere Pro offers various keyboard shortcuts that allow you to navigate between panels, toggle visibility, and perform common actions. These shortcuts contribute to a more efficient editing experience by reducing the time spent on manual panel navigation.

Conclusion:

Mastering the interface of Adobe Premiere Pro is a fundamental step towards becoming a proficient video editor. Understanding the purpose and function of each panel, customizing workspaces to suit your workflow, and arranging panels in a way that enhances your efficiency can drastically improve your editing experience. With a solid grasp of Premiere Pro's interface, you'll be better equipped to unleash your creativity and bring your video projects to life with precision and finesse. Whether you're a beginner or a seasoned professional, investing time in understanding and customizing the interface will undoubtedly pay off in the quality and efficiency of your video editing endeavors.

Importing media files: videos, audio, and images

In the realm of video editing, the process of importing media files lays the foundation for the creative journey that lies ahead. Adobe Premiere Pro, a powerhouse among video editing software, offers a seamless platform for importing a diverse range of media elements, from videos and audio clips to images. In this article, we will delve into the intricacies of importing these types of media files, exploring the tools and techniques that Premiere Pro provides to streamline the process and set the stage for captivating visual storytelling.

The Significance of Efficient Importing:
Efficiently importing media files is paramount to a smooth and productive video editing workflow. When assembling a video project, editors need access to a variety of assets, such as raw footage, soundtracks, graphics, and images. Premiere Pro's robust importing capabilities ensure that these elements can be seamlessly integrated into the project, allowing editors to focus on the creative aspects of their work without being hindered by technical challenges.

Importing Videos:
1. **File Navigation:** To import videos, open the Project panel and use the Import command to navigate to the location of your video files on your computer or external storage. You can also use the shortcut Ctrl + I (Cmd + I on Mac) for quick access.

2. **Selecting Multiple Files:** Premiere Pro supports batch importing, enabling you to select multiple video files to import at once. This is particularly helpful when dealing with a series of clips from a single shoot.

3. **Creating Bins:** Upon importing, you can organize your videos by creating bins (folders) in the Project panel. This helps keep your media assets neatly categorized, making them easier to locate during the editing process.

Importing Audio:
1. **Audio Formats:** Premiere Pro supports a wide range of audio formats, including WAV, MP3, AIFF, and more. Importing audio follows a similar process to importing videos.

2. **Syncing Audio and Video:** If you're working with separate audio and video files, Premiere Pro offers tools to help you sync them effortlessly. This is crucial for ensuring that audio remains perfectly aligned with the corresponding video footage.

3. **Importing Music and Sound Effects:** When adding background music or sound effects to your project, the same importing process applies. You can create bins to organize your audio assets just as you would with video.

Importing Images:
1. **Supported Formats:** Premiere Pro supports a wide range of image formats, including JPEG, PNG, GIF, and more. Images are often used for creating title cards, overlays, and graphics within your videos.

2. **Image Dimensions:** Pay attention to the dimensions of the images you import, as they will impact the quality and composition of your video. Images that are too small may appear pixelated when scaled up.

3. **Maintaining Aspect Ratios:** When importing images, ensure that they maintain the same aspect ratio as your video sequence to avoid distortion.

Conclusion:

Importing media files is the foundational step that sets the stage for creative exploration in Adobe Premiere Pro. The software's user-friendly interface and diverse importing capabilities empower editors to seamlessly integrate videos, audio, and images into their projects. By leveraging features like batch importing, organizing assets in bins, and syncing audio and video, editors can focus on the artistic aspects of video editing without being encumbered by technical hurdles.

As you embark on your video editing journey, understanding the nuances of importing media files is essential for achieving a polished and professional end product. Adobe Premiere Pro's robust importing features are designed to cater to the diverse needs of editors, whether they are working on a short film, a promotional video, or an educational tutorial. Ultimately, mastering the art of importing sets the tone for an efficient and creative editing process, allowing you to craft engaging visual narratives that resonate with your audience.

Navigating the timeline and basic editing tools

As you dive into the world of video editing using Adobe Premiere Pro, one of the first frontiers you'll encounter is the timeline. The timeline serves as the canvas upon which you weave your creative vision into a cohesive and captivating video. In this article, we'll explore the art of navigating the timeline and delve into the fundamental editing tools that Premiere Pro offers, empowering you to craft videos that tell stories, evoke emotions, and leave lasting impressions.

The Timeline: Where Creativity Takes Shape:
At the heart of Adobe Premiere Pro lies the timeline, a visual representation of your video project's sequence. It's here that you'll assemble your clips, audio tracks, effects, and transitions to craft your narrative. Navigating the timeline effectively is crucial for maintaining the flow of your video and bringing your ideas to life.

Understanding the Basics of the Timeline:
1. **Layers and Tracks:** The timeline is divided into layers, or tracks, each corresponding to a different element of your video. Common tracks include Video, Audio, Titles, and Effects. These tracks allow you to layer and synchronize various elements to create a harmonious composition.

2. **Adding Clips:** To add clips to the timeline, simply drag and drop them from the Project panel. Video clips go to the Video track, audio to the Audio track, and so on.

3. **Timeline Indicator:** The timeline indicator, often referred to as the playhead, marks the current position in your timeline. It's a crucial tool for navigating your project and making precise edits.

Basic Editing Tools: Crafting Your Narrative:
1. **Cutting and Trimming:** The razor tool (C) is your go-to for cutting clips in the timeline. You can make precise cuts at specific points to trim and rearrange clips seamlessly.

2. **Selection Tool:** The selection tool (V) allows you to select and move clips within the timeline. This tool is vital for arranging clips in the desired sequence.

3. **Ripple Edit Tool:** The ripple edit tool (B) is a time-saving gem. When you shorten or extend a clip, the adjacent clips automatically adjust to accommodate the change.

4. **Rolling Edit Tool:** The rolling edit tool (N) enables you to adjust the edit point between two clips. This tool is handy when you want to

alter the timing of a cut without affecting the overall length of the sequence.

Creating a Fluid Narrative:
Navigating the timeline and utilizing these basic editing tools opens the door to crafting a fluid narrative. Seamlessly cutting clips, arranging them in sequence, and utilizing tools like transitions and effects can transform raw footage into a polished video that captures your audience's attention.

Keyboard Shortcuts for Efficiency:
Premiere Pro offers a multitude of keyboard shortcuts that expedite the editing process. Learning and utilizing these shortcuts can significantly enhance your efficiency, allowing you to focus more on your creative vision and less on manual tasks.

Conclusion:
The timeline is where the magic of video editing happens in Adobe Premiere Pro. Navigating this space effectively, understanding the various tracks and layers, and mastering the basic editing tools lay the foundation for creating captivating videos. Whether you're piecing together a short film, a vlog, a documentary, or a promotional video, the timeline serves as your creative playground where ideas take shape and stories unfold.

By becoming adept at using the timeline and basic editing tools, you'll gain the confidence to experiment, refine, and perfect your videos. As you continue your journey in video editing, remember that the timeline is more than a linear sequence of clips – it's a canvas where your creativity knows no bounds, and your storytelling prowess shines through each frame.

Creating a new project and setting project settings

Creating a new project in Adobe Premiere Pro marks the exciting starting point of your video editing venture. This initial step involves setting the stage for your creative journey by defining crucial parameters that will influence the look, feel, and technical aspects of your project. In this comprehensive article, we'll delve into the process of creating a new project, exploring the intricacies of setting project settings, and understanding how these choices impact your editing experience and final output.

Laying the Groundwork: Creating a New Project:
1. **Launching Premiere Pro:** Open Adobe Premiere Pro, and you'll be greeted by the Home screen. Here, you can choose to create a new project or open an existing one.

2. **Setting the Project Name and Location:** Start by giving your project a name and specifying the location where your project files will be saved. This organization is essential for keeping your project files accessible and well-structured.

3. **Selecting a Scratch Disk:** Premiere Pro uses scratch disks to store temporary files generated during the editing process. You can designate the location of these scratch disks to optimize performance and storage.

Setting Project Settings: The Canvas of Your Creativity:

1. **Editing Mode and Timebase:** The editing mode defines the base settings for your project, such as resolution and frame rate. For example, you might choose an editing mode like "1080p" with a timebase of 24 frames per second (fps).

2. **Video and Audio Display Formats:** These settings determine how timecode and audio sample rates are displayed. These choices can be based on regional broadcasting standards or personal preferences.

3. **Capture Format and Capture Channel:** If you're working with footage from tape-based sources, these settings influence the format and audio configuration used during capture.

4. **Capture Location and Scratch Disks:** Specify the location where captured media will be saved. It's crucial to choose a location with ample storage space.

5. **Renderer:** Choose a renderer based on your hardware and preferences. The "Mercury Playback Engine GPU Acceleration" option utilizes your graphics card for smoother playback and rendering.

6. **Audio Hardware:** Configure your audio input and output settings, including selecting your audio hardware for playback and recording.

Selecting a Preset: Optimizing Your Workflow:

Premiere Pro provides various presets tailored to specific video formats, resolutions, and broadcasting standards. These presets streamline the process by automatically configuring project settings to match your chosen output.

For instance, if you're creating content for online platforms like YouTube, you might choose a preset that aligns with the platform's recommended settings, ensuring your video meets their requirements.

Custom Settings: Tailoring to Your Vision:

While presets offer convenience, you can also opt for custom settings if your project requires specific configurations that aren't covered by presets. Custom settings allow you to define aspects like resolution, frame rate, audio channels, and more according to your unique vision.

Conclusion: Crafting Your Vision from the Ground Up:

Creating a new project and setting project settings in Adobe Premiere Pro is more than a technical process – it's the art of laying the foundation for your creative journey. The choices you make at this stage influence the technical quality, aesthetics, and efficiency of your editing experience. Whether you're crafting a short film, a vlog, a documentary, or a commercial, the project settings you choose will shape the canvas upon which your creative vision unfolds.

By understanding the intricacies of project settings and harnessing the power of presets and custom configurations, you're equipped to embark on a video editing venture that aligns perfectly with your goals. As you navigate the vast landscape of Premiere Pro's options, remember that every setting you choose is a brushstroke on the canvas of your creative masterpiece, bringing your vision to life with precision and authenticity.

Chapter 2: Building a Solid Foundation Exploring the different video formats and codecs

In the realm of modern video editing, understanding video formats and codecs is paramount. As you embark on your creative journey with Adobe Premiere Pro, you'll encounter a plethora of options that influence the quality, compatibility, and efficiency of your video projects. This article delves into the complex world of video formats and codecs, unraveling their significance, exploring their nuances, and equipping you with the knowledge to make informed choices that enhance your editing experience.

Understanding Video Formats: Unveiling the Basics:
A video format is essentially a file container that holds the video, audio, and sometimes metadata of your project. Different video formats have varying levels of compression, quality, and compatibility with different devices and platforms. In Adobe Premiere Pro, you have the flexibility to work with a wide range of formats to suit your specific needs.

The Role of Codecs: Deciphering Compression:
Within each video format, compression is handled by a codec, short for "coder-decoder." A codec encodes the video and audio data during export and decodes it during playback. Codecs are responsible for reducing the file size of videos while maintaining an

acceptable level of quality. However, the choice of codec can significantly impact the final output and editing process.

Common Video Formats and Their Significance:
1. **AVI (Audio Video Interleave):** While AVI is widely supported, it's not as efficient in terms of compression as newer formats. It's commonly used for legacy systems or specific purposes.

2. **MP4 (MPEG-4 Part 14):** MP4 is one of the most versatile and widely supported video formats. It's suitable for web streaming, mobile devices, and social media platforms.

3. **MOV (QuickTime):** Developed by Apple, MOV files offer high-quality compression and are often used for video editing, especially on Mac systems.

4. **WMV (Windows Media Video):** WMV is a format commonly associated with Windows systems. While it offers good compression, it may have limited compatibility on non-Windows platforms.

5. **MKV (Matroska):** MKV files provide excellent quality and support for various codecs. They're popular for sharing high-definition videos.

Essential Codecs: Balancing Quality and Size:

1. **H.264:** This codec is a workhorse for web streaming and video sharing platforms. It offers a balance between file size and quality, making it an industry standard for online content.

2. **H.265 (HEVC - High-Efficiency Video Coding):** H.265 provides better compression while maintaining quality, making it suitable for 4K and high-resolution videos.

3. **ProRes:** Developed by Apple, ProRes is known for its exceptional quality and efficient compression. It's a favorite among professional video editors.

4. **DNxHD and DNxHR:** These codecs are developed by Avid and offer high-quality compression, ideal for editing and post-production workflows.

Choosing the Right Format and Codec: Factors to Consider:

1. **Quality:** The level of quality you desire for your final output impacts your choice of format and codec. For high-quality projects, consider formats with minimal compression, like ProRes or DNxHD.

2. **Compatibility:** Think about where your video will be displayed or distributed. If it's for the web, H.264 or H.265 may be ideal. If you're working within a specific software ecosystem, consider formats that are optimized for those platforms.

3. **Editing Efficiency:** Formats like ProRes and DNxHD are known for their efficient editing performance. These "intermediate" codecs are less compressed and allow for smoother editing.

4. **File Size:** Compression is directly tied to file size. While high compression reduces file size, it can also impact image quality. Balancing compression and quality is crucial, especially for distribution and storage.

Conclusion: Navigating the Video Format Maze with Confidence:

Exploring video formats and codecs in Adobe Premiere Pro is akin to deciphering a digital language that shapes the very essence of your video projects. With a grasp of their significance, you're better equipped to make choices that align with your creative vision and distribution goals.

By understanding the nuances of various formats and codecs, you can tailor your choices to optimize quality, compatibility, and editing efficiency. Whether you're crafting a cinematic masterpiece, a vlog, a tutorial, or a promotional video, the right combination of format and codec ensures that your creative endeavors translate seamlessly across devices and platforms, captivating your audience with the richness of your storytelling.

Understanding resolution, frame rates, and aspect ratios

In the world of video editing, the concepts of resolution, frame rates, and aspect ratios are fundamental building blocks that influence how we perceive and experience visual content. As you embark on your creative journey with Adobe Premiere Pro, delving into the intricacies of these elements is essential for crafting videos that captivate and resonate with your audience. This comprehensive article explores the nuances of resolution, frame rates, and aspect ratios, shedding light on their significance, interactions, and the ways they shape your video projects.

Resolution: The Canvas of Clarity and Detail:
Resolution refers to the number of pixels that compose an image or video. It dictates the clarity, sharpness, and level of detail in your visuals. In Adobe Premiere Pro, you have the flexibility to work with various resolutions to match your project's requirements.

Common Resolution Standards:
1. **Standard Definition (SD):** SD typically encompasses resolutions like 720x480 (NTSC) and 720x576 (PAL). This resolution was prevalent before the rise of high-definition content.

2. **High Definition (HD):** HD resolutions include 1280x720 (720p) and 1920x1080 (1080p). HD offers enhanced clarity and is the standard for modern video content.

3. **4K Ultra HD:** With a resolution of 3840x2160, 4K delivers stunning detail and is ideal for projects that demand exceptional visual quality.

4. **8K and Beyond:** Resolutions like 7680x4320 (8K) are on the horizon, pushing the boundaries of visual fidelity even further.

Aspect Ratios: Framing Your Visual Narrative:
The aspect ratio represents the proportional relationship between a video's width and height. It influences how your visuals are framed and the storytelling impact they convey.

Common Aspect Ratios:
1. **16:9:** Also known as widescreen, 16:9 is the standard aspect ratio for modern content and

is commonly used for TVs, monitors, and online platforms.

2. **4:3:** This aspect ratio, once prevalent in older TVs, has given way to widescreen formats but is still used for specific purposes.

3. **1:1:** Square aspect ratios are popular on social media platforms like Instagram, providing a unique framing for creative expression.

4. **2.35:1 and 2.39:1:** These cinematic aspect ratios create a wide, panoramic look often associated with epic films.

Frame Rates: The Rhythm of Motion:
Frame rate refers to the number of individual frames (images) displayed per second in a video. It determines the smoothness of motion and the perception of realism.

Common Frame Rates:
1. **24 fps:** This cinematic frame rate is synonymous with the traditional film look and is often used for narrative filmmaking.

2. **30 fps:** A common frame rate for television and online content, offering a balance between smooth motion and visual quality.

3. **60 fps:** Higher frame rates, like 60 fps, provide smoother motion and are often used for action scenes and fast-paced videos.

4. **120 fps and Beyond:** Ultra-high frame rates are utilized for slow-motion effects, capturing details that might be missed at standard frame rates.

The Interaction Between Resolution, Aspect Ratios, and Frame Rates:
Understanding how resolution, aspect ratios, and frame rates interact is crucial for maintaining visual consistency and optimizing playback quality. When setting these parameters in Adobe Premiere Pro, consider the following:

1. **Resolution and Aspect Ratio:** Different resolutions may have associated aspect ratios. Ensure your chosen aspect ratio aligns with your intended visual framing.

2. **Frame Rate and Motion:** Higher frame rates create smoother motion but require more data. Choose a frame rate that suits your project's pace and style.

3. **Resolution and Performance:** Higher resolutions demand more processing power and storage. Consider your hardware

capabilities when working with 4K or higher resolutions.

Choosing the Right Combination for Your Project:
Selecting the appropriate resolution, aspect ratio, and frame rate is a delicate balance that hinges on your creative intent, distribution platform, and audience engagement. A cinematic film may benefit from the classic 24 fps frame rate, while a high-energy vlog might thrive with 60 fps for dynamic motion.

By understanding these core elements and their interactions, you're empowered to make informed decisions that align with your artistic vision and technical requirements. Adobe Premiere Pro's flexibility allows you to experiment, innovate, and craft videos that resonate deeply with your audience, enveloping them in the richness of your visual storytelling.

The role of project presets and sequence settings
In the realm of video editing, achieving visual consistency and seamless workflows is paramount. Enter project presets and sequence settings – two vital components in Adobe Premiere Pro that lay the foundation for your creative endeavors. In this comprehensive article, we'll delve into the significance of project presets and sequence settings, exploring how these settings influence your video projects, streamline your editing process, and

ultimately contribute to the polished and professional quality of your work.

Project Presets: Shaping Your Creative Space:
When you create a new project in Adobe Premiere Pro, you're presented with the opportunity to select a project preset. A project preset is a predefined configuration that determines your project's resolution, frame rate, and aspect ratio. It essentially sets the canvas on which your creative vision will come to life.

Customizing Project Presets:
Adobe Premiere Pro provides a range of built-in project presets tailored to common formats, resolutions, and frame rates. These presets serve as starting points for your projects and ensure that your settings align with your intended output. However, you also have the flexibility to create custom project presets that cater to your unique needs.

The Impact of Project Presets:
1. **Visual Consistency:** Selecting the appropriate project preset ensures visual consistency across all your sequences. If you're working on a series of videos, maintaining the same project preset ensures that each video adheres to a unified visual style.

2. **Efficiency:** Project presets streamline your editing process by automatically configuring

settings like resolution and frame rate. This eliminates the need to manually adjust these settings for every new project.

3. **Compatibility:** By choosing a project preset that matches your desired output platform, you ensure compatibility with various devices and platforms. Whether you're creating content for online streaming, broadcast, or social media, the right preset enhances playback quality and viewer experience.

Sequence Settings: Tailoring Your Canvas for Creativity:

Once you've set your project preset, you move on to creating sequences within your project. A sequence is essentially the timeline where you assemble your video clips, audio, and effects. Sequence settings allow you to fine-tune the technical aspects of your video editing canvas.

Selecting Sequence Settings:

When you create a new sequence, you have the option to choose from a variety of sequence presets. These presets define parameters such as resolution, frame rate, and audio settings specific to the type of content you're creating.

Custom Sequence Settings:
While sequence presets provide convenient starting points, you can also customize sequence settings to match your project's unique requirements. This is particularly useful if your project involves unconventional frame rates, resolutions, or audio configurations.

The Influence of Sequence Settings:
1. **Technical Precision:** Sequence settings ensure that your video and audio components align seamlessly. Choosing the correct settings prevents issues like audio-video synchronization problems or distortion.

2. **Editing Flexibility:** By selecting the appropriate sequence settings, you optimize your canvas for efficient editing. Proper settings enhance playback performance, allowing you to edit smoothly without lag or rendering delays.

3. **Output Quality:** Sequence settings significantly impact the final output quality of your video. Selecting settings that align with your project's intended distribution platform ensures that your video is displayed at its best.

Balancing Creative Vision and Technical Precision:
The delicate balance between creative vision and technical precision is where project presets and sequence settings shine. While the technical aspects ensure a seamless editing experience and optimal output quality, they also provide a framework for your artistic expression. These settings empower you to focus on storytelling, composition, and visual impact while knowing that the technical foundation is strong. In Adobe Premiere Pro, mastering project presets and sequence settings is essential for achieving professional-quality videos. Whether you're crafting short films, documentaries, tutorials, or promotional content, understanding how these settings work in harmony enhances your editing efficiency, elevates your visual storytelling, and ensures that your videos resonate deeply with your audience.

Organizing your media assets using bins and folders
In the dynamic world of video editing, the ability to efficiently manage your media assets is a skill that separates the organized from the chaotic. Adobe Premiere Pro provides a robust organizational system through the use of bins and folders. These tools empower you to maintain a structured workspace, streamline your editing process, and navigate your project with ease. This comprehensive article explores the significance of organizing media assets, the functionalities of bins and folders, and how these tools contribute to the success of your creative endeavors.

The Importance of Organizing Media Assets:

Imagine embarking on a video editing journey armed with a plethora of video clips, audio files, images, and graphics. Without a well-organized system, finding the right asset at the right time can be a daunting task. Organizing your media assets offers several key benefits:

1. **Efficiency:** Organized assets expedite the editing process. Instead of spending time searching for files, you can focus on crafting your narrative.

2. **Visual Consistency:** Grouping related assets ensures that you maintain visual consistency throughout your project. This is particularly important for elements like title cards, graphics, and B-roll.

3. **Collaboration:** Organized assets enhance collaboration among team members. A structured system allows everyone to access and work with the same resources.

Understanding Bins and Folders:

In Adobe Premiere Pro, bins and folders are the cornerstone of your organizational structure. Think of bins as containers that hold related assets, and folders as a way to further categorize and group these bins.

Creating Bins:
1. **Project Panel:** Open the Project panel in Adobe Premiere Pro. Right-click in the panel and select "New Bin." Give your bin a descriptive name, such as "Footage," "Graphics," or "Sound Effects."

2. **Drag and Drop:** You can also create bins by dragging and dropping assets into the Project panel. Premiere Pro automatically prompts you to create a new bin to hold the imported assets.

Creating Folders:
1. **Organizing Bins:** Right-click in the Project panel and select "New Bin." After creating the bin, you can drag and drop other bins into it, creating a folder-like structure.

2. **Subfolders:** To create subfolders within folders, follow a similar process. Right-click, select "New Bin," and then drag and drop it into the desired parent folder.

The Art of Categorization:
Effective categorization is key to maintaining an organized workspace. Consider the nature of your project and the types of assets you're working with. Here are some common categories to consider:

1. **Footage:** Store your video clips here, organized by scenes, locations, or shooting dates.

2. **Audio:** Group your audio files, including music tracks, sound effects, and voiceovers.

3. **Graphics:** Store graphics, title cards, lower-thirds, and other visual elements here.

4. **Sequences:** Create a bin to house your sequences. This keeps your timeline organized and your project panel clutter-free.

Benefits of Organizing with Bins and Folders:
1. **Ease of Access:** Organized bins and folders provide a clear path to finding specific assets when you need them.

2. **Quick Navigation:** With a structured system, you can quickly locate and import assets into your timeline.

3. **Efficient Editing:** Organized assets enhance your editing flow, allowing you to focus on creativity rather than searching for files.

4. **Consistency:** A well-organized workspace ensures consistent visual elements and sound throughout your project.

Conclusion: The Art of Organized Creativity:

As a video editor, your canvas is not just the timeline – it's also the meticulously structured bins and folders that house your media assets. The art of organizing your media assets using bins and folders in Adobe Premiere Pro transforms the chaos of raw files into a canvas of creative potential. By curating a systematic environment, you set the stage for smoother workflows, enhanced collaboration, and a seamless editing experience. Your media assets become accessible tools that empower you to craft compelling narratives, tell captivating stories, and create videos that resonate deeply with your audience.

Chapter 3: Essential Editing Techniques
Cutting and trimming clips in the timeline

Video editing is a craft that involves precision, creativity, and a keen eye for detail. One of the fundamental skills in this creative journey is the art of cutting and trimming clips within the timeline. Adobe Premiere Pro, a versatile and powerful editing tool, provides a plethora of tools and techniques to help you shape your raw footage into a cohesive and engaging visual story. In this comprehensive article, we'll delve into the intricacies of cutting and trimming clips in the Adobe Premiere Pro timeline, exploring the tools at your disposal, the strategies you can employ, and the impact these skills have on your final video production.

Understanding Cutting and Trimming: The Building Blocks of Editing:

At the heart of video editing lies the ability to manipulate clips, rearranging them to create a seamless flow that captures your intended narrative. Cutting involves removing sections of a clip to isolate the desired content, while trimming refers to adjusting the in and out points of clips to fine-tune their timing.

Tools for Cutting and Trimming:

Adobe Premiere Pro offers a range of tools to facilitate cutting and trimming:

1. **Razor Tool (C):** The razor tool allows you to make precise cuts in clips. Simply position the razor tool at the desired point in the timeline and click to split the clip.

2. **Selection Tool (V):** The selection tool is used to select and move clips in the timeline. It's vital for rearranging your sequence and ensuring a coherent flow.

3. **Trimming Tools:** These tools include the Ripple Edit tool (B), Rolling Edit tool (N), and Rate Stretch tool (R). They enable you to adjust the length of clips while maintaining synchronization with adjacent clips.

Cutting Clips: Craftsmanship in Action:
1. **Razor Tool Usage:** To cut a clip using the razor tool, place the tool at the desired cut point and click. This splits the clip into two segments.

2. **Removing Unwanted Portions:** Delete the unwanted portion of the clip by selecting it and pressing the Delete key. This effectively trims the clip to the desired length.

Trimming Clips: Sculpting Visual Timing:
1. **Ripple Edit Tool (B):** This tool adjusts the length of a clip while simultaneously adjusting

adjacent clips to maintain synchronization. It's useful when you want to change the duration of a clip without creating gaps in your timeline.

2. **Rolling Edit Tool (N):** The rolling edit tool shifts the edit point between two adjacent clips. It's valuable when you want to alter the timing of a cut without changing the overall length of the sequence.

3. **Rate Stretch Tool (R):** The rate stretch tool changes the speed of a clip, allowing you to speed up or slow down its playback without affecting its duration on the timeline.

The Art of Seamless Transitions:
Cutting and trimming are not just technical processes; they're also about achieving smooth transitions that enhance your storytelling. Properly executed cuts and trims create a visual rhythm that guides your audience's attention and emotions.

Precision and Creativity:
Cutting and trimming are both technical and creative skills. The precision of your cuts and the finesse of your trims impact the overall pacing, rhythm, and emotional resonance of your video.

Conclusion: Elevating Your Video Editing Craft:
In the world of video editing, the mastery of cutting and trimming is the hallmark of a skilled editor. Adobe Premiere Pro equips you with a suite of tools and techniques to transform raw footage into a polished narrative. By understanding the dynamics of cuts, trims, and transitions, you're empowered to shape your videos with precision, creativity, and an acute awareness of visual storytelling. As you navigate the intricacies of the timeline and refine your cutting and trimming techniques, you'll find yourself not just editing clips, but crafting an immersive and captivating visual experience that resonates deeply with your audience.

Using the razor tool for precise cuts

Video editing is an art of precision – a delicate dance between clips, transitions, and storytelling. At the forefront of this creative journey lies the razor tool, a potent instrument within Adobe Premiere Pro's toolkit that empowers editors to make surgical cuts with exacting precision. In this comprehensive article, we will dive into the world of the razor tool, exploring its functionalities, techniques, and the impact it has on your editing prowess. By harnessing the power of the razor tool, you'll uncover new horizons in your video editing, transforming raw footage into a visual masterpiece.

Unveiling the Razor Tool: A Keen Edge in Video Editing:

The razor tool is a tool of surgical precision, enabling editors to split clips precisely where desired. Its versatility lies in its ability to create clean cuts, extract segments, and sculpt your narrative with finesse. The razor tool is not merely a utility; it's a creative weapon that empowers you to shape your story and enhance the flow of your video.

Accessing the Razor Tool:

You can access the razor tool in Adobe Premiere Pro by simply pressing the 'C' key on your keyboard or selecting it from the toolbar. When activated, the cursor transforms into a razor icon, ready to make precise incisions in your timeline.

The Art of Precise Cuts: Techniques and Strategies:

1. **Single Cut:** Click on the desired point in the timeline where you wish to make a cut. The razor tool creates a clear divide in the clip, allowing you to extract or rearrange segments as needed.

2. **Multiple Cuts:** To create multiple cuts in a single clip, hold down the Shift key while clicking at various points along the timeline. This technique is useful for dissecting a clip into smaller sections.

3. **Removing Unwanted Portions:** Once you've made your cuts, use the selection tool ('V') to

select the portion you wish to remove. Press the Delete key to eliminate the selected segment, leaving behind a seamless edit.

Precision and Continuity: The Razor Tool's Role in Seamless Edits:

The razor tool plays a pivotal role in maintaining continuity within your video. Precise cuts ensure that there are no abrupt jumps or disruptions in the visual flow. By understanding the nuances of the razor tool, you can seamlessly remove unwanted portions, create smooth transitions, and weave together a narrative that flows effortlessly.

Crafting Visual Rhythms: Enhancing Pacing and Timing:

Beyond the technical aspect, the razor tool aids in crafting visual rhythms that dictate the pacing and timing of your video. It allows you to sync cuts with beats of music, emphasize dramatic moments, and control the tempo of your storytelling. Each cut becomes a brushstroke on the canvas of your creative vision, contributing to the overall composition and emotional impact of your video.

The Razor Tool: A Key to Creative Control:

The razor tool is not a mere utility for making cuts; it's a gateway to creative control over your video's structure, pacing, and visual impact. By mastering the art of using the razor tool in Adobe Premiere Pro, you unlock the ability to transform raw footage into a coherent, engaging, and visually captivating narrative.

Conclusion: Precision as Your Creative Signature:
In the realm of video editing, the razor tool is your chisel, your scalpel – a tool that allows you to sculpt your raw footage into a polished masterpiece. Its precision empowers you to make cuts that align with your creative intent, guiding your audience's attention and emotions. As you explore the capabilities of the razor tool, you'll find yourself not just making cuts, but imprinting your creative signature on each frame, each transition, and each moment of your video.

Understanding the basics of transitions and applying them

Video editing is a delicate interplay of visuals, emotions, and narrative flow. At the heart of this artistic endeavor lies the concept of transitions – a vital element that connects scenes, enhances storytelling, and engages the audience. Adobe Premiere Pro, a powerhouse of video editing software, offers a diverse array of transition options that allow editors to weave a seamless tapestry of visual continuity. In this comprehensive article, we'll delve into the fundamentals of transitions, explore their significance, and uncover the techniques for applying them effectively to elevate your video projects to new heights.

Demystifying Transitions: The Link Between Scenes:
Transitions are tools that bridge the gap between two distinct scenes or shots. They help maintain the flow of your video by guiding the viewer's eye and emotions from one moment to the next. Transitions can vary from subtle cuts to dynamic animations, each serving a unique purpose in enhancing the visual storytelling.

Types of Transitions: A World of Possibilities:
Adobe Premiere Pro offers an array of transitions to suit various creative needs:

1. **Cut:** The simplest and most direct transition, the cut involves switching abruptly from one shot to the next. It's effective for maintaining a fast pace or creating contrast between scenes.

2. **Dissolve/Fade:** This transition gradually fades from one shot to another, creating a smooth blend between scenes. Dissolves are commonly used to indicate the passage of time or evoke a dreamy atmosphere.

3. **Wipe:** A wipe transition reveals the new shot by pushing or wiping away the previous shot. This technique can add a touch of novelty and creativity to your edits.

4. **Slide:** The slide transition moves one shot off the screen to reveal the next. It's ideal for

showcasing comparisons or revealing hidden elements.

5. **Zoom:** The zoom transition creates the illusion of zooming in or out of a shot, enhancing the visual impact and drawing attention to specific details.

6. **Crossfade:** Also known as a cross dissolve, this transition smoothly blends two shots by gradually fading one out while fading the other in. It's a staple for creating seamless transitions between scenes.

Applying Transitions: Techniques for Fluidity:
1. **Drag-and-Drop:** In Adobe Premiere Pro's Effects panel, find the desired transition, then drag and drop it onto the edit point between two clips in the timeline.

2. **Effect Controls:** After applying a transition, you can access its parameters in the Effect Controls panel. Here, you can adjust duration, alignment, and other settings to customize the transition's appearance.

3. **Preview and Adjust:** It's essential to preview transitions in the context of your project. This helps you gauge their timing, impact, and overall effectiveness.

Strategies for Effective Transition Use:

1. **Contextual Relevance:** Choose transitions that align with the tone, genre, and mood of your video. A horror film might benefit from sharp cuts, while a romantic montage may call for gentle dissolves.

2. **Storytelling Enhancements:** Transitions can enhance storytelling by emphasizing moments of change, surprise, or emotional intensity. Use them strategically to guide your audience's emotions.

3. **Avoid Overuse:** While transitions are powerful tools, using too many can disrupt the natural flow of your video. Prioritize clarity and coherence over excessive visual flair.

Conclusion: Elevating Your Narrative with Flawless Transitions:

Transitions are the threads that weave your visual narrative into a cohesive tapestry. By understanding the basics of transitions and their various types, you gain the power to guide your audience's journey, enhance emotional impact, and create a polished visual experience. Adobe Premiere Pro's versatile transition options empower you to create captivating videos that seamlessly transport viewers from scene to scene, ensuring that your storytelling resonates deeply and lingers long after the final frame.

Adding and manipulating audio tracks

In the world of video editing, audio is not just an accompanying element – it's a powerful tool that shapes the emotional resonance and immersive quality of your visual storytelling. Adobe Premiere Pro, a creative haven for video editors, offers an array of features that allow you to add, manipulate, and fine-tune audio tracks to perfection. This comprehensive article delves into the art of audio editing within Adobe Premiere Pro, exploring the process of adding audio tracks, adjusting levels, applying effects, and orchestrating a harmonious symphony that complements your visual narrative.

The Symphony of Audio Tracks: An Integral Component of Video Editing:
Audio is more than just background noise; it's an essential layer that deepens the viewer's engagement with your video. The combination of dialogue, music, sound effects, and ambient noise creates an auditory landscape that enhances the emotional impact of your story.

Adding Audio Tracks: Setting the Stage:
Adobe Premiere Pro provides a user-friendly interface for adding audio tracks to your timeline:
1. **Importing Audio:** Start by importing your audio files into the Project panel. You can drag

and drop them directly from your computer or use the "Import" command.

2. **Creating Audio Tracks:** In the timeline, right-click to create a new audio track. Choose the desired number of channels – mono, stereo, or multi-channel – based on your audio source.

3. **Dragging and Dropping:** Drag your imported audio files onto the newly created audio track in the timeline.

Manipulating Audio Tracks: Crafting the Perfect Blend:

1. **Volume Adjustment:** Adjusting audio levels is fundamental to creating a balanced mix. In Adobe Premiere Pro, you can use the audio track's volume rubber band to raise or lower the volume at specific points.

2. **Keyframes:** For more precise control over volume changes, you can use keyframes. By adding keyframes to the volume rubber band and adjusting their positions, you can create gradual fades, dynamic changes, and intricate audio dynamics.

3. **Audio Effects:** Adobe Premiere Pro offers a wide range of audio effects that can be applied to individual clips or entire tracks. These effects include equalization (EQ), reverb, compression, and more. Effects can be used to

enhance audio clarity, create specific moods, or simulate environmental conditions.

Syncing Audio and Visuals: Achieving Synchronization:

1. **Audio Waveforms:** Adobe Premiere Pro displays audio waveforms in the timeline, allowing you to identify visual cues that match with audio beats, dialogue, or actions.

2. **Markers and Cues:** Utilize markers and cue points to synchronize audio with specific visual events. This is especially useful for aligning music beats with impactful moments in your video.

Working with Multiple Audio Tracks: Crafting Complexity:

1. **Layered Soundscapes:** Multiple audio tracks allow you to create complex soundscapes by layering different elements. Dialogue, background music, ambient sounds, and sound effects can all coexist on separate tracks.

2. **Audio Mixing:** Mixing involves balancing the levels of different audio tracks to create a cohesive auditory experience. Adobe

Premiere Pro's audio mixer panel provides a visual representation of your audio tracks, allowing you to adjust levels, apply effects, and monitor output in real time.

Exporting the Final Audio: Capturing the Essence:
When your audio tracks are finely tuned, it's time to export your project while preserving the audio quality:

1. **Export Settings:** In the Export Settings window, ensure that your audio settings match your desired output format. You can choose various audio codecs and bitrates based on your distribution platform.

2. **Bit Depth and Sample Rate:** Depending on the project requirements, you can adjust the bit depth (16-bit or 24-bit) and sample rate (typically 44.1 kHz or 48 kHz) to maintain optimal audio quality.

Conclusion: Orchestrating Audio Excellence in Adobe Premiere Pro:
Adding and manipulating audio tracks in Adobe Premiere Pro is not just a technical process; it's an art form that enhances the impact of your video. By seamlessly integrating dialogue, music, sound effects, and ambient noise, you create an auditory landscape

that complements and elevates your visual narrative. Adobe Premiere Pro's array of tools and features provide the canvas on which you craft a symphony of sounds, harmonizing the senses and enveloping your audience in an immersive experience that resonates deeply and lingers long after the final frame fades.

Chapter 4: Enhancing Your Video with Effects and Transitions
Working with video and audio effects

Video editing is not just about assembling footage; it's about transforming raw content into a compelling visual journey that captivates and resonates with your audience. A significant part of this transformation lies in the realm of video and audio effects – tools that allow you to manipulate visuals and sounds to enhance storytelling, evoke emotions, and create a dynamic viewing experience. Adobe Premiere Pro, a treasure trove of creative possibilities, offers an array of video and audio effects that empower editors to add layers of creativity and finesse to their projects. This comprehensive article delves into the world of video and audio effects, exploring their applications, techniques, and the ways in which they contribute to the magic of video editing.

The Art of Visual and Sonic Transformation:
Video and audio effects are not just technical enhancements; they're artistic tools that shape the mood, tone, and impact of your video. Visual effects can transport viewers to fantastical realms, while audio effects can immerse them in rich soundscapes. Understanding how to work with these effects is key to unlocking a world of creative possibilities.

Video Effects: Transforming Visuals with Finesse:

1. **Accessing Video Effects:** In Adobe Premiere Pro, you can access video effects through the Effects panel. This panel offers a vast library of effects, each with its unique attributes and applications.

2. **Drag and Drop Application:** To apply a video effect, simply drag and drop it onto the desired clip in the timeline. Once applied, the effect can be further customized using the Effect Controls panel.

3. **Layering Effects:** You can apply multiple effects to a single clip, creating a layered effect that combines various visual enhancements.

Types of Video Effects: Enhancing Visual Storytelling:
1. **Color Correction:** Video effects like color grading and correction allow you to adjust the color balance, saturation, and contrast of your clips. This is crucial for establishing the mood and atmosphere of your video.

2. **Transitions:** Transitions go beyond simple cuts, adding dynamic movement between shots. Cross dissolves, wipes, and zooms are just a few examples of transitions that enhance visual continuity.

3. **Visual Filters:** Filters such as blur, sharpen, and vignette can be applied to create specific visual effects. These filters alter the look and feel of your footage, from dreamy to dramatic.

Audio Effects: Shaping Sonic Landscapes:

1. **Accessing Audio Effects:** Similar to video effects, audio effects can be accessed through the Effects panel. Applying audio effects to audio clips enhances their sound quality and emotional impact.

2. **Equalization (EQ):** EQ effects allow you to adjust the balance of different frequencies in audio. This is useful for enhancing clarity, removing noise, and emphasizing specific elements.

3. **Reverb and Echo:** Reverb and echo effects add a sense of space and depth to audio clips, simulating environments and enhancing the auditory experience.

4. **Compression:** Compression evens out the dynamic range of audio, making loud sounds softer and soft sounds louder. This effect is used to create a balanced and polished audio mix.

Techniques for Creative Application: Crafting Visual and Sonic Excellence:

1. **Subtle Enhancements:** Sometimes, less is more. Subtle application of effects can elevate your video without overwhelming the viewer.

2. **Theme Alignment:** Choose effects that align with the theme and genre of your video. Effects should enhance the narrative, not distract from it.

3. **Keyframing:** Keyframes allow you to apply effects over time. For example, you can gradually change the color tone of a clip or pan the audio from left to right.

Previewing and Rendering: The Importance of Quality Control:

Before finalizing your project, it's crucial to preview your effects and render them for optimal playback quality:

1. **Previewing:** Adobe Premiere Pro allows you to preview effects in real time. This helps you gauge their impact on your project's overall visual and auditory experience.

2. **Rendering:** Once you're satisfied with the effects, render your project to ensure smooth playback. Rendering converts your timeline

into a format that can be played back seamlessly.

Conclusion: Unleashing Creative Brilliance with Effects:

Video and audio effects are the brushstrokes that add depth, texture, and emotion to your video canvas. By understanding the nuances of these effects and their applications, you gain the power to craft an immersive visual and auditory experience that captivates and resonates with your audience. Adobe Premiere Pro's extensive library of effects, combined with your creative vision, enables you to elevate your video projects from mere sequences of clips to captivating narratives that leave a lasting impression. As you navigate the world of video and audio effects, you're not just editing – you're transforming raw footage into a masterpiece of visual and sonic excellence.

Applying color correction and grading

In the realm of visual storytelling, color is a potent language that communicates emotions, sets moods, and guides the viewer's gaze. Harnessing the power of color correction and grading in video editing is akin to wielding a painter's palette – a skill that transforms raw footage into a vivid, evocative canvas. Adobe Premiere Pro, a realm of creative possibilities, offers a suite of tools and techniques for applying color correction and grading, allowing editors to shape the visual tone, atmosphere, and narrative impact of their videos. This comprehensive article delves into the art of color correction and grading, exploring their nuances, methodologies, and the transformative role they play in the cinematic experience.

Color as the Unseen Narrator: Understanding Color Correction and Grading:

Color correction and grading are not merely technical processes; they're the heartbeats of visual storytelling. Color correction involves correcting inconsistencies in color and exposure, while grading is the artistic process of enhancing, altering, and stylizing the colors to convey a specific mood or aesthetic.

The Tools of the Trade: Adobe Premiere Pro's Color Grading Capabilities:

Adobe Premiere Pro offers a robust toolkit for color correction and grading:

1. **Lumetri Color Panel:** This panel provides a comprehensive range of color correction and grading tools, making it a one-stop destination for color manipulation.

2. **Color Wheels:** The three-way color wheels allow you to adjust shadows, midtones, and highlights individually. This is essential for achieving accurate color balance.

3. **Curves:** Curves provide fine control over the brightness and contrast of specific tonal ranges, allowing for nuanced adjustments.

4. **Creative LUTs:** Look-Up Tables (LUTs) are preset color profiles that alter the colors of your footage. They're used to achieve specific cinematic styles and aesthetics.

The Art of Color Correction: Balancing the Visual Equation:
1. **Exposure Correction:** Begin by correcting exposure issues, ensuring that your highlights are not blown out and your shadows retain detail.

2. **White Balance:** Adjust the white balance to neutralize color casts caused by different lighting conditions. This brings a sense of realism to your footage.

3. **Skin Tone Enhancement:** Accurate skin tones are vital for maintaining a natural look. Use the color wheels to fine-tune skin tones, making them lifelike and appealing.

Color Grading: The Creative Alchemy:
1. **Setting the Mood:** Color grading is where creativity takes center stage. By manipulating

colors, you can create distinct moods – warm tones for nostalgia, cool tones for tension, and vibrant tones for energy.

2. **Contrast and Saturation:** Enhance contrast and adjust saturation to add depth and richness to your visuals. These adjustments bring your footage to life and draw attention to specific elements.

3. **Using LUTs:** LUTs are powerful tools for achieving cinematic looks. Apply a LUT to your footage and then fine-tune it using other color grading tools for a personalized touch.

Color Consistency: The Thread That Binds:
1. **Maintaining Consistency:** Consistency is crucial, especially in multi-shot sequences. Use adjustment layers to apply color corrections or grading to multiple clips at once, ensuring visual harmony.

2. **Shot Matching:** Adobe Premiere Pro offers automated shot matching tools that analyze color and lighting across clips to achieve visual coherence.

Mastering the Visual Language: The Impact of Color Correction and Grading:

The choices you make in color correction and grading directly influence your video's narrative impact:

1. **Visual Storytelling:** Colors can enhance character emotions, highlight narrative elements, and signify transitions or changes in mood.

2. **Atmosphere and Tone:** The choice of color can establish the time of day, the climate, and the overall atmosphere of your scenes.

3. **Aesthetic Identity:** Color grading establishes your video's visual identity. Consistent color choices contribute to a cohesive and professional look.

Conclusion: Crafting Cinematic Brilliance:

Color correction and grading are the finishing touches that elevate your video from ordinary to extraordinary. Adobe Premiere Pro's color manipulation tools offer a creative playground where you can shape moods, enhance storytelling, and create visual spectacles that resonate deeply with your audience. As you navigate the world of color correction and grading, you're not just editing; you're painting with light and color, crafting a visual experience that lingers in the hearts and minds of viewers. By mastering the art of color correction and grading, you become the architect of cinematic brilliance, infusing every frame with intention, emotion, and creative flair.

Creating dynamic motion with keyframes

Motion breathes life into still images, infusing them with energy, emotion, and narrative flow. In the world of video editing, this dynamic motion is achieved through the magic of keyframes – a creative tool that empowers editors to orchestrate movement, transitions, and visual storytelling within Adobe Premiere Pro. In this comprehensive article, we'll dive deep into the realm of keyframes, exploring their significance, techniques, and the ways they transform static footage into a vibrant visual journey that captivates and engages the audience.

Keyframes: Unveiling the Essence of Motion:

Keyframes are the building blocks of motion in video editing. They are individual frames that mark the beginning or end of an animation or change in visual attributes over time. By setting keyframes at specific intervals, editors can animate properties like position, scale, opacity, and more, effectively bringing images to life.

Accessing Keyframes in Adobe Premiere Pro:

Adobe Premiere Pro provides a user-friendly interface for working with keyframes:

1. **Effects Controls Panel:** Open the Effects Controls panel to view the keyframe options

for the selected clip or effect. Here, you can adjust parameters and set keyframes.

2. **Stopwatch Icons:** Keyframes are represented by stopwatch icons next to adjustable properties. Clicking the stopwatch adds a keyframe at the current time indicator.

Animating Properties: Crafting Dynamic Motion:
1. **Position and Scale:** Moving and scaling images are fundamental animation techniques. By setting keyframes for position and scale properties, you can create smooth transitions and dynamic movement.

2. **Opacity:** Adjusting opacity through keyframes can fade images in or out, or create subtle transitions between clips.

3. **Rotation:** Rotating images using keyframes adds a dynamic spin to your animations, enhancing visual interest.

4. **Effects and Filters:** Many effects and filters in Adobe Premiere Pro can be animated using keyframes. This includes effects like blur, color correction, and even text animations.

Techniques for Mastering Keyframe Animation:
1. **Ease In and Ease Out:** To create smooth animations, apply ease in (gradual

acceleration) and ease out (gradual deceleration) to your keyframes. This prevents abrupt starts and stops in motion.

2. **Speed Variation:** Varying the speed between keyframes adds a sense of realism to your animations. For example, a subtle slowdown at the end of a pan creates a natural feeling of momentum.

3. **Linear vs. Bezier Keyframes:** Bezier keyframes offer more control over animation curves. You can adjust their handles to manipulate the speed and trajectory of the animation.

Animating Text and Graphics: Adding Depth and Dimension:

1. **Text Animation:** Applying keyframes to text attributes like position, scale, and opacity can create captivating text animations that emphasize points, reveal messages, or enhance storytelling.

2. **Graphics and Titles:** Keyframes can transform static graphics into dynamic elements. By animating parameters like position, scale, and rotation, you can infuse graphics with movement and energy.

Complex Animations: Layering and Nesting:
1. **Nested Sequences:** For more complex animations, consider creating nested sequences. This involves placing multiple clips and effects within a single sequence, allowing for intricate animations.

2. **Layering Effects:** By layering multiple effects with keyframe animations, you can create intricate visuals that evolve over time. This is particularly useful for creating transitions or visual effects.

Preview and Refinement: The Art of Iteration:
1. **Real-Time Preview:** Adobe Premiere Pro offers a real-time preview of keyframe animations. Use this feature to gauge the pacing, timing, and visual impact of your animations.

2. **Iterative Refinement:** Crafting dynamic motion with keyframes is an iterative process. Preview your animation, make adjustments, and fine-tune until you achieve the desired effect.

Conclusion: The Symphony of Dynamic Motion:

Keyframes are the conductor's baton in the symphony of video editing. By mastering the art of keyframe animation in Adobe Premiere Pro, you become the orchestrator of dynamic motion, guiding your audience's gaze, evoking emotions, and enhancing the overall visual experience. Each keyframe is a brushstroke on the canvas of time, transforming static images into a mesmerizing dance that captivates and enchants. As you explore the possibilities of keyframe animation, you're not just editing – you're crafting a visual spectacle that transports viewers to new dimensions, immersing them in a dynamic world where every frame tells a story.

Adding and customizing transitions for seamless cuts

Video editing is a craft of transitions – the art of seamlessly connecting scenes, guiding the viewer's gaze, and enhancing the narrative flow. Adobe Premiere Pro, a haven for creative storytellers, offers a wide array of transitions that transform mundane cuts into captivating visual experiences. In this comprehensive article, we will embark on a journey through the realm of transitions, exploring their importance, techniques for adding and customizing them, and the role they play in creating a cohesive and engaging video narrative.

The Power of Transitions: Stitching the Fabric of Visual Storytelling:

Transitions are more than just eye candy; they're narrative tools that facilitate the fluid movement between scenes. Whether subtle or dynamic, transitions ensure that your video maintains its rhythm, captivates the audience, and sustains their emotional engagement.

Accessing Transitions in Adobe Premiere Pro: A Gateway to Creativity:

1. **Effects Panel:** In Adobe Premiere Pro, transitions are accessible through the Effects panel. Here, you'll find a plethora of transition options to choose from.

2. **Drag and Drop:** To apply a transition, simply drag and drop it between two clips in the timeline. This creates a transition effect that seamlessly connects the two shots.

Types of Transitions: Shaping the Visual Tone:

1. **Cut:** The most straightforward transition, a cut involves an immediate shift from one shot to another. It's effective for maintaining a brisk pace or creating stark visual contrast.

2. **Dissolve/Fade:** The dissolve transition gradually fades from one shot to another, creating a smooth blending effect. This is often

used to indicate the passage of time or evoke a dreamy atmosphere.

3. **Wipe:** A wipe transition reveals the new shot by pushing or wiping away the previous shot. It adds a dynamic element to your video and can be creatively customized.

4. **Slide:** A slide transition moves one shot off-screen to reveal the next. This technique is useful for showing comparisons or revealing hidden elements.

5. **Zoom:** A zoom transition creates the illusion of zooming in or out of a shot, engaging the viewer and drawing attention to specific details.

Customizing Transitions: Infusing Personal Flair:
1. **Duration and Timing:** Adjust the duration of your transitions to control the pace of the switch between shots. Longer transitions evoke a slower, contemplative mood, while shorter ones maintain a swift rhythm.

2. **Ease In and Ease Out:** Apply easing to your transitions to create a natural acceleration and deceleration of the transition effect. This prevents abrupt cuts and adds a touch of realism.

3. **Effect Controls:** Use the Effect Controls panel to fine-tune your transitions. Depending on the transition type, you can adjust parameters like direction, angle, and specific visual attributes.

Creating Custom Transition Effects: Crafting Originality:

1. **Video Effects:** Combine video effects with transitions to create unique visual transitions. For example, a blur effect can be used to create a dreamy transition between shots.

2. **Text and Graphics:** Overlaying text or graphics during a transition adds an extra layer of storytelling. This is particularly effective for introducing new scenes or emphasizing specific elements.

Previewing and Fine-Tuning: The Art of Perfection:

1. **Real-Time Preview:** Adobe Premiere Pro offers a real-time preview of transitions. This feature allows you to see how the transitions play out in the context of your video.

2. **Fine-Tuning:** Preview your transitions and make adjustments as needed. Pay attention to the timing, visual appeal, and overall

coherence of the transitions within the video sequence.

Conclusion: The Elegance of Seamless Transitions:
Transitions are the threads that bind the fabric of your video narrative. With Adobe Premiere Pro's diverse transition options and customization features, you have the tools to elevate your storytelling to new heights. By applying and customizing transitions thoughtfully, you guide your audience through an immersive visual journey that flows seamlessly, capturing their attention and evoking emotions at every turn. As you delve into the art of transitions, you're not just editing; you're crafting a symphony of visuals that harmonize, captivate, and linger in the minds of viewers, ensuring your video is an unforgettable tapestry of cinematic excellence.

Chapter 5: Advanced Editing Tools and Techniques
Utilizing the multi-camera editing feature

The world of video production is constantly evolving, offering filmmakers and content creators innovative tools to tell their stories in more engaging and dynamic ways. One such tool that has transformed the landscape of video editing is the multi-camera editing feature. With Adobe Premiere Pro at the forefront of creative software, editors can harness the power of multi-camera editing to seamlessly stitch together footage from different angles, capturing every moment, every perspective, and every emotion. In this comprehensive article, we'll dive deep into the realm of multi-camera editing, exploring its importance, techniques for utilizing the feature effectively, and the ways it enhances the visual narrative.

Understanding Multi-Camera Editing: The Essence of Dynamic Storytelling:
Multi-camera editing is not just about stitching together multiple video feeds; it's about creating a dynamic visual experience that immerses the audience in the heart of the action. This feature is especially valuable for projects with multiple cameras capturing the same event from different viewpoints.

Accessing Multi-Camera Editing in Adobe Premiere Pro: A Gateway to Creativity:

1. **Creating a Multi-Camera Source Sequence:** Start by right-clicking on the selected footage in the Project panel and choosing "Create Multi-Camera Source Sequence." This action opens the Multi-Camera Source Sequence dialog box.

2. **Syncing and Aligning Clips:** Adobe Premiere Pro offers various methods to synchronize and align your clips. You can use timecode, audio cues, or markers to ensure seamless syncing.

Multi-Camera Editing Techniques: Crafting a Unified Visual Experience:

1. **Switching Camera Angles:** In the Multi-Camera Monitor panel, you can switch between different camera angles by simply clicking on the desired angle. This allows you to select the most appropriate shots for different moments in the video.

2. **Adding Cuts:** During playback, add cuts by pressing the "C" key or clicking the camera icons in the Multi-Camera Monitor panel. These cuts create edit points where the camera angles switch.

3. **Creating Edit Points:** As you add cuts, Adobe Premiere Pro automatically creates edit points on the Multi-Camera Source Sequence

timeline. These edit points define the moments when camera angles switch.

Fine-Tuning Multi-Camera Edits: The Art of Precision:
1. **Switching Modes:** Adobe Premiere Pro offers several modes for multi-camera editing, including "Toggle Multi-Camera View" and "Multi-Camera Editing." Experiment with these modes to find the most comfortable workflow.

2. **Real-Time Playback:** Utilize the Multi-Camera Monitor's real-time playback feature to preview your edits and ensure a seamless flow between camera angles.

3. **Editing the Sequence:** After creating the Multi-Camera Source Sequence, you can further refine and edit the sequence like any other timeline in Adobe Premiere Pro. Add transitions, effects, and audio adjustments to enhance the overall quality.

Syncing Audio and Fine-Tuning Sound:
1. **Audio Syncing:** Multi-camera editing often involves multiple audio sources. Use audio syncing methods to ensure that audio from different cameras aligns seamlessly.

2. **Audio Mixing:** Adobe Premiere Pro's audio mixing tools allow you to balance audio levels, eliminate background noise, and enhance overall sound quality.

Creating Multi-Camera Sequences: Expanding the Visual Landscape:

1. **Nested Sequences:** For more complex projects, consider creating nested sequences. This involves turning your Multi-Camera Source Sequence into a nested sequence within a larger project, enabling further editing and enhancement.

2. **Layering Effects:** By layering effects, transitions, and graphics onto your multi-camera sequence, you can add depth, dimension, and visual interest to your video.

Previewing and Refinement: Achieving Perfection:

1. **Real-Time Preview:** Adobe Premiere Pro's real-time preview feature is a valuable tool for evaluating the flow and impact of your multi-camera edits. Use it to fine-tune the timing and pacing.

2. **Iterative Refinement:** Multi-camera editing is an iterative process. Preview your edits, make

adjustments, and refine until you achieve the desired visual and narrative impact.

Conclusion: Elevating Storytelling with Multi-Camera Magic:

Multi-camera editing is a gateway to crafting dynamic and immersive video narratives. With Adobe Premiere Pro's multi-camera editing feature, you have the tools to seamlessly integrate footage from multiple angles, enriching the visual experience and providing viewers with a front-row seat to the action. As you explore the nuances of multi-camera editing, you're not just assembling footage; you're weaving a tapestry of perspectives, emotions, and moments into a compelling visual journey. By mastering the art of multi-camera editing, you transform video production into a cinematic spectacle, capturing the essence of every angle and ensuring that your audience is captivated from the first frame to the last.

Exploring the power of the nested sequences

Video editing is a multi-dimensional art form that thrives on the interplay of visuals, sound, and storytelling. Nested sequences, a versatile feature in Adobe Premiere Pro, provide editors with a powerful tool to elevate their projects to new heights of creativity and organization. By delving into the realm of nested sequences, you unlock the ability to layer, manipulate, and streamline your editing process, leading to more intricate narratives, polished visuals, and seamless workflows. In this comprehensive article, we'll dive deep into the world of nested sequences, exploring their significance, techniques for creating and using them effectively, and the ways they enhance the overall quality of your video projects.

Understanding Nested Sequences: The Essence of Composition and Organization:
At its core, a nested sequence is a sequence within a sequence. This concept allows you to break down your project into manageable components, giving you more control over editing, effects, and transitions. Nested sequences facilitate a modular approach, allowing you to work on different elements separately while maintaining cohesion in the final video.

Accessing Nested Sequences in Adobe Premiere Pro: A Gateway to Creativity:

1. **Creating Nested Sequences:** To create a nested sequence, select the clips you want to include and right-click. Choose "Nest" from the context menu, and Adobe Premiere Pro will create a new sequence containing your selected clips.

2. **Opening Nested Sequences:** Double-clicking on a nested sequence in the Project panel opens it as a separate timeline. You can then

edit the contents of the nested sequence just like you would in the main timeline.

Advantages of Using Nested Sequences: Enhanced Workflow and Creativity:

1. **Organizational Benefits:** Nested sequences streamline the editing process by allowing you to focus on specific elements without cluttering the main timeline. This leads to a more organized workspace.

2. **Efficient Editing:** Nested sequences enable more efficient editing, as you can work on different sections of your project separately and then bring them together seamlessly.

3. **Layered Effects and Transitions:** By applying effects and transitions to a nested sequence, you can create more intricate visual effects that are consistent throughout the video.

Creating Multi-Camera Sequences with Nested Sequences: A Deeper Dive:

1. **Multi-Camera Editing:** We've discussed multi-camera editing earlier; nested sequences take this concept further. By creating a nested sequence for each camera angle, you can edit

and switch between them with ease in the main sequence.

2. **Editing Flexibility:** Nested sequences offer flexibility in multi-camera editing, allowing you to make changes to individual angles while preserving the overall structure of the video.

Applying Effects to Nested Sequences: Elevating Visuals:

1. **Effects on Nested Sequences:** Apply effects to a nested sequence to create a unified look or enhance specific segments of your video. This is especially useful for color grading, audio adjustments, and visual enhancements.

2. **Transitions and Animation:** By applying transitions and animation to a nested sequence, you can create complex visual sequences that play out seamlessly.

Nested Sequences for Montages and Flashbacks: Storytelling Mastery:

1. **Montages:** Nested sequences are a powerful tool for creating montages. Compile various clips into a nested sequence, allowing you to edit and refine the montage independently.

2. **Flashbacks and Flash-forwards:** Use nested sequences to create seamless transitions between the present and past or future, enhancing the narrative flow and visual storytelling.

Previewing and Refinement: Achieving Visual Excellence:
1. **Real-Time Preview:** Adobe Premiere Pro's real-time preview feature helps you evaluate the effects, transitions, and overall flow of your nested sequences within the context of the main timeline.

2. **Iterative Refinement:** Nested sequences allow for iterative refinement. Preview your sequences, make adjustments, and fine-tune until you achieve the desired visual and narrative impact.

Conclusion: Crafting Complexity with Nested Sequences:
Nested sequences are the toolbox for intricate storytelling and visual finesse. With Adobe Premiere Pro's nested sequence feature, you gain the power to compose, refine, and layer your video projects with greater precision and creativity. As you explore the capabilities of nested sequences, you're not just

editing; you're sculpting narratives, enhancing visuals, and orchestrating a symphony of elements that captivate and engage your audience. By mastering the art of nested sequences, you transform video editing into a multi-dimensional art form, crafting videos that resonate deeply and linger in the minds of viewers long after the final frame fades.

Mastering the art of audio editing and mixing

While visuals capture the eyes, it's the power of sound that immerses viewers in the world of storytelling. Audio editing and mixing are the unsung heroes of video production, the elements that elevate narratives from ordinary to extraordinary. Adobe Premiere Pro, a hub of creative possibilities, offers a comprehensive suite of tools for shaping, refining, and perfecting audio. In this comprehensive article, we'll delve into the art of audio editing and mixing, exploring techniques for crafting captivating soundscapes, achieving balance, and infusing your videos with professional-grade audio that resonates deeply.

The Role of Audio Editing and Mixing: Crafting Sonic Narratives:
Audio is more than just background noise; it's a narrative tool that adds depth, emotion, and atmosphere to your videos. Effective audio editing and mixing enhance storytelling, guide emotional responses, and create a richer viewing experience.

Accessing Audio Editing and Mixing Tools in Adobe Premiere Pro: A Symphony of Possibilities:

1. **Audio Track Mixer:** The Audio Track Mixer in Adobe Premiere Pro is your control center for audio mixing. It allows you to adjust volume, panning, and apply effects to individual tracks.

2. **Audio Effects:** Adobe Premiere Pro offers a wide range of audio effects that can be applied to individual clips or entire tracks. These effects include EQ, compression, reverb, and more.

Audio Editing Techniques: Sculpting Soundscapes:

1. **Removing Background Noise:** Clean audio is essential. Use noise reduction tools to eliminate unwanted background noise and enhance the clarity of dialogue and narration.

2. **Adjusting Volume Levels:** Balance audio levels to ensure dialogue is clear and music or effects don't overpower the narration. Use keyframes to create smooth transitions between different volume levels.

3. **Cutting and Trimming:** Like video editing, audio editing involves precise cuts and trims. Remove unnecessary pauses, breaths, or mistakes to maintain a smooth flow.

4. **Time Stretching and Pitch Shifting:** Adjusting the tempo or pitch of audio clips can help sync audio with video or create dramatic effects.

Audio Mixing Techniques: Achieving Sonic Harmony:
1. **Balancing Audio Levels:** The key to effective mixing is achieving a balance between different audio elements. Use the Audio Track Mixer to adjust levels so that nothing is too loud or too quiet.

2. **Panning:** Panning adjusts the placement of sound within the stereo field. This adds depth and directionality to your audio, enhancing the immersive experience.

3. **Equalization (EQ):** EQ adjusts the balance of frequencies in audio. Use EQ to enhance clarity, remove unwanted frequencies, and achieve a balanced mix.

4. **Compression:** Compression evens out the dynamic range of audio, making loud sounds softer and soft sounds louder. This creates a polished and consistent mix.

Adding Depth with Audio Effects: Elevating Soundscapes:

1. **Reverb:** Reverb adds a sense of space to audio, making it sound as if it's in a specific environment. Use reverb to create realistic or dramatic effects.

2. **Delay:** Delay creates echoes, adding texture and depth to audio. It's commonly used to make vocals stand out or create a sense of distance.

3. **Special Effects:** Adobe Premiere Pro's audio effects library includes a variety of tools to create unique sonic experiences. Experiment with effects like flanger, chorus, and distortion.

Achieving Sync and Timing: The Art of Precision:

1. **Lip Sync and ADR:** Ensure that dialogue matches lip movements precisely. Automated Dialogue Replacement (ADR) can be used to re-record and sync dialogue for seamless integration.

2. **Music and Sound Effects:** Sync music and sound effects to match the visuals. Use keyframes to adjust volume levels and create impactful audio cues.

Previewing and Fine-Tuning: The Quest for Perfection:

1. **Real-Time Preview:** Adobe Premiere Pro's real-time preview feature helps you evaluate audio edits and mixing decisions within the context of the video.

2. **Listening Sessions:** Regularly listen to your audio on different devices to ensure it sounds good across a variety of platforms and environments.

Conclusion: Weaving Sonic Tapestries with Precision:
Audio editing and mixing are the threads that weave the tapestry of your video narrative. With Adobe Premiere Pro's powerful audio tools, you have the ability to sculpt soundscapes that enhance storytelling, evoke emotions, and transport viewers into the heart of your video. As you explore the intricacies of audio editing and mixing, you're not just working with sound; you're creating an auditory symphony that resonates deeply and lingers in the minds of your audience. By mastering the art of audio editing and mixing, you elevate your videos from visual spectacles to immersive sensory experiences, ensuring that every frame is accompanied by audio that captivates, engages, and leaves a lasting impression.

Creating and animating text and titles

In the realm of video production, text and titles are more than just words on a screen – they're visual elements that convey information, set the tone, and enhance the narrative. Adobe Premiere Pro, a playground of creative possibilities, offers a comprehensive toolkit for creating and animating text and titles that add depth, style, and professionalism to your videos. In this comprehensive article, we'll delve into the art of text and title creation, exploring techniques for designing captivating typography, animating titles with finesse, and infusing your videos with dynamic visual storytelling.

The Power of Text and Titles: Words that Illuminate the Screen:

Text and titles are not mere captions; they're a part of the visual language that guides the viewer through your video. Well-designed text and titles reinforce your message, create visual interest, and provide context to the unfolding story.

Accessing Text and Title Tools in Adobe Premiere Pro: The Canvas of Creativity:

1. **Essential Graphics Panel:** The Essential Graphics panel in Adobe Premiere Pro is your gateway to creating, editing, and animating text and titles. Here, you'll find a range of text options and controls.

2. **Text Tool:** The Text tool allows you to create text layers directly on the timeline. Click and drag to define the text box, and start typing your content.

Text Creation Techniques: Crafting Visually Appealing Typography:

1. **Font Selection:** Choose fonts that complement the video's style and theme. Serif fonts convey tradition and seriousness, while sans-serif fonts evoke modernity and simplicity.

2. **Hierarchy and Readability:** Prioritize readability by using font sizes, weights, and colors to establish a clear hierarchy. Make sure titles are easily legible on various devices.

3. **Text Styles:** Experiment with bold, italics, underline, and other text styles to emphasize key points and add visual variety.

4. **Text Animation Presets:** Adobe Premiere Pro offers a variety of text animation presets that apply dynamic animations with a single click. These presets save time and add flair to your titles.

Animating Text and Titles: Breathing Life into Typography:

1. **Keyframing Text Animation:** Keyframes are the heart of text animation. By setting keyframes for attributes like position, scale, rotation, and opacity, you can create smooth and dynamic text animations.

2. **Motion Paths:** Use motion paths to animate text along a specified trajectory. This technique is particularly effective for adding movement to titles that follow a specific path.

3. **Text Reveals:** Create engaging title reveals by animating the appearance of text. This can involve fades, wipes, or even intricate animations that build anticipation.

Text Animation Techniques: Crafting Engaging Visual Narratives:

1. **Kinetic Typography:** Kinetic typography adds a layer of motion to text, creating a captivating visual experience. Use keyframes to choreograph text movements that align with the rhythm of the video.

2. **Emphasis and Timing:** Use text animations to emphasize key moments or phrases. Time text animations with the pacing of the video to create impactful visual cues.

3. **Transitions and Interaction:** Animate text transitions to introduce new sections or emphasize changes in narrative. Consider using text animations to interact with visual elements, enhancing the overall engagement.

Previewing and Fine-Tuning: The Quest for Perfection:
1. **Real-Time Preview:** Adobe Premiere Pro's real-time preview feature allows you to see how text animations play out within the context of your video.

2. **Listening Sessions:** Regularly review and fine-tune text animations, ensuring they align with the narrative flow and visual aesthetics of the video.

Conclusion: Crafting Visual Poetry with Text and Titles:
Text and titles are the visual poetry that accompanies your video's imagery. With Adobe Premiere Pro's rich text and title tools, you have the ability to craft dynamic, animated typography that enhances storytelling, captivates viewers, and reinforces your message. As you explore the world of text and title creation and animation, you're not just arranging words; you're designing visual narratives that engage, inform, and resonate deeply. By mastering the art of

text and title animation, you elevate your videos from simple recordings to dynamic visual spectacles, where every word dances across the screen, adding rhythm, meaning, and impact to your cinematic journey.

Chapter 6: Working with Audio
Importing and editing audio tracks

In the realm of video production, sound is a crucial element that transports viewers into the heart of the narrative. Captivating audio tracks complement visuals, evoke emotions, and create a truly immersive experience. Adobe Premiere Pro, a haven for creative storytellers, offers a comprehensive set of tools for importing and editing audio tracks that elevate your videos to new heights of sonic excellence. In this comprehensive article, we'll delve into the art of importing and editing audio tracks, exploring techniques for seamlessly integrating sound, enhancing audio quality, and crafting captivating auditory narratives.

The Power of Audio Tracks: Enhancing Visual Narratives with Sound:

Audio tracks are the soul of your video – they enrich storytelling, evoke emotions, and immerse viewers in the world you've created. Whether it's dialogue, music, or sound effects, each audio element contributes to the overall impact of your video.

Importing Audio Tracks in Adobe Premiere Pro: A Gateway to Sonic Creativity:

1. **Media Browser:** The Media Browser in Adobe Premiere Pro is your portal to importing audio tracks. Browse your media files, locate the

desired audio, and simply drag it into your project.

2. **Import Dialog:** Use the "Import" option from the File menu to browse and select audio files. This method provides additional options for managing the import settings.

Audio Editing Techniques: Shaping Soundscapes with Precision:

1. **Trimming and Cutting:** Similar to video editing, audio editing involves precise cuts and trims. Use the "Razor" tool to split audio clips and remove unwanted sections.

2. **Volume Adjustment:** Balance audio levels by adjusting the volume of individual clips. Ensure that dialogue is clear and music doesn't overpower narration.

3. **Audio Transitions:** Apply audio transitions to smoothen the transition between different audio clips. Crossfades and fade-ins/fade-outs create seamless auditory shifts.

Enhancing Audio Quality: The Quest for Sonic Excellence:

1. **Noise Reduction:** Clean audio is essential. Use noise reduction tools to remove background

noise and improve the clarity of dialogue and narration.

2. **Equalization (EQ):** EQ adjusts the balance of frequencies in audio. Enhance clarity by boosting the important frequencies and attenuating unwanted ones.

3. **Compression:** Compression evens out the dynamic range of audio, making loud sounds softer and soft sounds louder. This creates a polished and consistent mix.

Syncing Audio and Video: Achieving Perfect Harmony:
1. **Clapperboard and Sync Marks:** When recording, use visual cues like clapperboards or sync marks to ensure that audio and video are in sync. This makes editing much easier.

2. **Audio Waveforms:** Visualize audio waveforms in Adobe Premiere Pro to align audio clips precisely with video cues. Zoom in to accurately match audio with visual moments.

Applying Effects to Audio: Elevating Soundscapes with Creativity:
1. **Audio Effects:** Adobe Premiere Pro's audio effects library offers a range of creative tools.

Apply effects like reverb, delay, and modulation to add depth and dimension.

2. **Audio Keyframing:** Keyframe audio effects to create dynamic changes over time. For instance, gradually increasing the reverb on a voice can simulate a character's thoughts.

Previewing and Fine-Tuning: The Quest for Sonic Perfection:
1. **Real-Time Preview:** Adobe Premiere Pro's real-time preview feature helps you evaluate audio edits within the context of your video. Listen for clarity, balance, and overall impact.

2. **Listening Sessions:** Regularly review and fine-tune audio tracks on different devices to ensure a consistent listening experience across various platforms.

Conclusion: Crafting Immersive Auditory Landscapes:
Importing and editing audio tracks is akin to painting with sound, infusing your video with emotions, atmosphere, and depth. With Adobe Premiere Pro's versatile audio tools, you have the means to craft captivating soundscapes that complement visuals, enhance storytelling, and immerse viewers in a truly multi-sensory experience. As you explore the

intricacies of audio editing, you're not just fine-tuning; you're composing auditory symphonies that resonate deeply and linger in the minds of your audience. By mastering the art of importing and editing audio tracks, you transform video production into a sonic journey, where every note, every sound effect, and every whisper enriches the narrative tapestry, creating videos that are not just seen, but felt and heard on a profound level.

Applying audio effects and filters

In the realm of video production, audio effects and filters are the secret ingredients that transform raw audio into immersive soundscapes. These sonic enhancements elevate storytelling, evoke emotions, and add depth to the viewer's experience. Adobe Premiere Pro, a treasure trove of creative tools, offers a vast array of audio effects and filters that allow you to sculpt, shape, and refine your audio tracks. In this comprehensive article, we'll delve into the art of applying audio effects and filters, exploring techniques for enhancing audio quality, creating dynamic auditory experiences, and weaving intricate auditory narratives.

The Impact of Audio Effects and Filters: Sculpting Sonic Realities:
Audio effects and filters are the brushstrokes that paint the auditory canvas of your video. They create mood, atmosphere, and texture, guiding the

audience's emotional response and adding a layer of depth to the visual narrative.

Accessing Audio Effects and Filters in Adobe Premiere Pro: Your Sonic Toolkit:

1. **Effects Panel:** The Effects panel in Adobe Premiere Pro is your hub for accessing a wide range of audio effects and filters. Here, you'll find tools to transform your audio tracks and create unique auditory experiences.

2. **Audio Effects:** Adobe Premiere Pro offers a diverse library of audio effects and filters, including EQ, reverb, delay, compression, distortion, and more. These tools are essential for shaping audio to fit your creative vision.

Audio Effects Techniques: Elevating Auditory Excellence:

1. **Equalization (EQ):** EQ is a fundamental tool for adjusting the balance of frequencies in your audio. Enhance clarity by boosting important frequencies and attenuating unwanted ones.

2. **Reverb and Ambience:** Reverb adds a sense of space to audio, simulating different environments. Choose from various reverb presets or customize settings to create specific acoustic effects.

3. **Delay and Echo:** Delay creates echoes, adding texture and depth to audio. Use delay to simulate distance or to create dramatic effects that enhance the emotional impact.

4. **Compression:** Compression evens out the dynamic range of audio, making loud sounds softer and soft sounds louder. This creates a polished and consistent audio mix.

5. **Distortion and Saturation:** Apply distortion or saturation to create unique tonal qualities. This is particularly useful for adding warmth or grit to audio, such as simulating vintage recordings.

Audio Filters Techniques: Crafting Sonic Narratives:

1. **High-Pass and Low-Pass Filters:** High-pass filters remove low-frequency rumble, while low-pass filters remove high-frequency noise. Use these filters to clean up audio and achieve a cleaner mix.

2. **Notch Filters:** Notch filters target specific frequencies and reduce unwanted resonances or hums. This is valuable for eliminating background noises like electrical interference.

3. **Pitch Shift and Time Stretch:** Alter the pitch and time of audio using these filters. This can

be used for creative effects or to match audio to video cues.

Creative Approaches: Elevating Soundscapes with Artistry:

1. **Layering Effects:** Combine multiple effects to create complex and rich audio textures. For example, combining reverb with delay can simulate a vast, echoing space.

2. **Automating Effects:** Keyframe audio effects to create dynamic changes over time. Gradually increasing or decreasing an effect's intensity can enhance dramatic moments or transitions.

Real-Time Preview and Fine-Tuning: Crafting Sonic Perfection:

1. **Real-Time Preview:** Adobe Premiere Pro's real-time preview feature helps you evaluate the impact of audio effects within the context of your video. Listen for nuances, balance, and overall impact.

2. **Listening Sessions:** Regularly review and fine-tune audio effects on different devices to ensure a consistent auditory experience across various platforms.

Conclusion: Mastering the Sonic Canvas:
Applying audio effects and filters is the art of crafting auditory masterpieces that complement and enhance your visual storytelling. With Adobe Premiere Pro's extensive library of tools, you have the power to shape audio tracks into immersive soundscapes that captivate, engage, and resonate deeply with your audience. As you explore the realm of audio effects and filters, you're not just enhancing sound; you're creating a symphony of emotions, atmospheres, and textures that envelop your viewers in a sensory journey. By mastering the art of applying audio effects and filters, you elevate video production to a multisensory experience, ensuring that every sound, every note, and every effect adds richness, depth, and impact to your visual narratives.

Adjusting audio levels and creating a balanced mix

In the world of video production, audio levels and balance are the keys to crafting a captivating auditory experience. Well-adjusted audio levels and a balanced mix ensure that dialogue is clear, music is engaging, and sound effects resonate with impact. Adobe Premiere Pro, a realm of creative possibilities, offers a comprehensive toolkit for adjusting audio levels and achieving sonic equilibrium that enriches your videos. In this comprehensive article, we'll delve into the art of adjusting audio levels, creating a balanced mix, and infusing your videos with dynamic auditory narratives.

The Essence of Audio Levels and Balance: Elevating Soundscapes:

Audio levels and balance are the architects of your auditory landscape. They orchestrate the interplay between different audio elements, ensuring that each sound is heard with clarity and purpose.

Accessing Audio Levels and Balancing Tools in Adobe Premiere Pro: Your Sonic Console:

1. **Audio Track Mixer:** The Audio Track Mixer in Adobe Premiere Pro is your control center for adjusting audio levels and achieving a balanced mix. It's here that you can fine-tune every aspect of your audio.

2. **Audio Clip Mixer:** The Audio Clip Mixer focuses on adjusting audio levels and balance on a clip-by-clip basis, offering precision control over individual audio elements.

Adjusting Audio Levels Techniques: Sculpting Sound with Precision:

1. **Volume Control:** Use the faders in the Audio Track Mixer or Audio Clip Mixer to adjust the volume of each audio track or clip. Balance different audio elements to ensure clarity and impact.

2. **Keyframing Volume:** For precise control over audio levels, keyframe volume changes over

time. Gradual increases or decreases can enhance narrative moments or transitions.

3. **Automation Modes:** Adobe Premiere Pro offers various automation modes, including "Read," "Write," and "Latch." These modes allow you to record volume changes in real time or manually adjust them.

Achieving a Balanced Mix: The Sonic Equation:
1. **Dialogue Clarity:** Ensure that dialogue is clear and intelligible. Adjust other audio elements to prevent dialogue from getting lost in the mix.

2. **Music Dynamics:** Balance music levels to support the emotional tone of the video. Gradually increase or decrease music volume to underscore dramatic moments.

3. **Sound Effects Impact:** Elevate the impact of sound effects by adjusting their levels. Make sure they're prominent enough to be heard without overwhelming the other audio elements.

Panning: Shaping the Sonic Landscape:
1. **Pan Control:** Adjust pan controls in the Audio Track Mixer or Audio Clip Mixer to position

audio within the stereo field. This creates a sense of direction and space.

2. **Stereo and Mono Balance:** Balance stereo and mono audio sources to achieve consistency in the auditory experience. Ensure that neither type overpowers the other.

Previewing and Fine-Tuning: The Quest for Sonic Excellence:

1. **Real-Time Preview:** Adobe Premiere Pro's real-time preview feature helps you evaluate audio adjustments within the context of your video. Listen for balance, clarity, and overall impact.

2. **Listening Sessions:** Regularly review and fine-tune audio levels on different devices to ensure a consistent auditory experience across various platforms.

Creating Audio Mix Presets: Crafting Consistency and Efficiency:

1. **Saving Mix Presets:** Once you've achieved a balanced mix that suits your project, save it as a mix preset. This allows you to apply the same mix settings to multiple projects.

2. **Recalling Mix Presets:** In future projects, simply load your saved mix presets to quickly achieve a balanced audio mix without starting from scratch.

Conclusion: Crafting Sonic Narratives with Precision: Adjusting audio levels and creating a balanced mix is the art of sculpting auditory landscapes that complement and elevate your visual storytelling. With Adobe Premiere Pro's powerful audio tools, you have the means to shape audio elements into harmonious compositions that captivate, engage, and resonate with your audience. As you explore the intricacies of audio levels and balance, you're not just fine-tuning; you're creating auditory symphonies that immerse your viewers in a multisensory experience. By mastering the art of adjusting audio levels and creating a balanced mix, you transform video production into a sensory journey, where every sound, every note, and every rhythm adds richness, depth, and impact to your cinematic narratives.

Syncing audio and video for perfect alignment

In the realm of video production, the synchronization of audio and video is paramount. When audio and video are perfectly aligned, the viewer's immersion is seamless, storytelling is enhanced, and the overall impact of the content is maximized. Adobe Premiere Pro, a realm of creative possibilities, offers a range of tools and techniques to achieve precise audio and video synchronization. In this comprehensive article, we'll delve into the art of syncing audio and video, exploring methods for ensuring perfect alignment, overcoming common challenges, and infusing your videos with a harmonious and immersive experience.

The Essence of Audio and Video Synchronization: Crafting Seamless Narratives:
Audio and video synchronization is the invisible thread that weaves together the visual and auditory elements of your video. It ensures that actions, dialogue, and sounds align perfectly, creating a natural and engaging viewing experience.

Accessing Synchronization Tools in Adobe Premiere Pro: Your Temporal Canvas:
1. **Timeline View:** The timeline in Adobe Premiere Pro serves as your temporal canvas, where you arrange and synchronize audio and video tracks to create a cohesive narrative.

2. **Timecode and Audio Waveforms:** Utilize timecodes and audio waveforms to visually identify points of synchronization. Waveforms display the peaks and valleys of audio, making it easier to match actions and dialogue with video cues.

Synchronization Techniques: Achieving Flawless Alignment:

1. **Clapperboards and Sync Marks:** During filming, use clapperboards or visual sync marks to create distinct audio and visual cues. These cues serve as synchronization points during the editing process.

2. **Audio Waveform Matching:** Align audio waveforms with visual cues on the timeline. Zoom in for precise adjustments, ensuring that actions and speech are perfectly matched to their corresponding moments.

3. **Timecode Alignment:** Use timecodes to match specific moments between audio and video tracks. Adjust the starting points to synchronize both elements accurately.

Overcoming Common Challenges: A Guide to Precision:

1. **Variable Frame Rates:** If your video was shot with variable frame rates, you may encounter synchronization issues. Convert the footage to a constant frame rate before editing to ensure accurate alignment.

2. **Lip Sync and ADR:** Achieving accurate lip sync is crucial for natural dialogue. If needed, use Automated Dialogue Replacement (ADR) to

rerecord and synchronize speech for seamless alignment.

3. **Footage and Audio Drift:** Over long shots or extended scenes, footage and audio may drift out of sync due to technical factors. Regularly check for drift and make necessary adjustments.

Fine-Tuning and Precision: The Quest for Synchronization Perfection:
1. **Keyframing Audio and Video:** When working with separate audio and video tracks, keyframe adjustments allow you to fine-tune synchronization on a granular level.

2. **Listening and Viewing Sessions:** Regularly review audio and video synchronization on different devices and platforms to ensure a consistent experience for your audience.

Using Markers and In and Out Points: Crafting Synchronization Landmarks:
1. **Markers:** Mark specific synchronization points on the timeline to guide your editing process. Markers help you remember critical moments that require alignment.

2. **In and Out Points:** Use in and out points to define the portions of audio and video that need synchronization. This allows you to focus on specific segments without altering the entire timeline.

Real-Time Preview: Listening and Watching in Unison:

1. **Real-Time Preview:** Adobe Premiere Pro's real-time preview feature helps you evaluate synchronization adjustments within the context of your video. Listen and watch for seamless alignment.

2. **A/B Comparisons:** Use the A/B comparison feature to toggle between different synchronization points and evaluate which alignment works best for the scene.

Conclusion: Crafting Seamless Experiences:

Synchronizing audio and video is the art of crafting a seamless sensory experience that elevates your visual storytelling. With Adobe Premiere Pro's array of tools, you have the means to align actions, dialogue, and sounds with precision, creating a cohesive and immersive viewing journey. As you explore the intricacies of audio and video synchronization, you're not just aligning elements; you're orchestrating a symphony of visuals and sound that captivates, engages, and resonates deeply with your audience. By mastering the art of synchronizing audio and video, you transform video production into a harmonious experience where every gesture, every word, and every sound aligns perfectly, creating videos that are not just seen and heard, but felt and experienced on a profound level.

Chapter 7: Exporting and Sharing Your Work
Understanding export settings and formats

In the world of video production, the final export is the culmination of creative efforts, transforming raw footage and intricate edits into a polished and shareable masterpiece. Adobe Premiere Pro, a realm of creative possibilities, provides a multitude of export settings and formats that enable you to tailor your video output for various platforms, devices, and purposes. In this comprehensive article, we'll delve into the art of understanding export settings and formats, exploring techniques for achieving optimal video quality, selecting the right settings, and ensuring your videos shine across different screens.

The Significance of Export Settings and Formats: Transforming Vision into Reality:
Export settings and formats are the bridge between your creative process and the audience's experience. The choices you make during export determine how your video will look, sound, and perform on different devices and platforms.

Accessing Export Settings in Adobe Premiere Pro: Your Gateway to Perfection:
1. **Export Window:** The Export window in Adobe Premiere Pro is your gateway to customizing export settings. Here, you'll find a plethora of options to fine-tune your output to meet your specific needs.

2. **Preset Selection:** Adobe Premiere Pro offers preset export settings for various platforms and devices, such as YouTube, Vimeo, and mobile devices. These presets simplify the export process and ensure compatibility.

Choosing the Right Export Settings: Balancing Quality and File Size:
1. **Resolution and Frame Rate:** Select a resolution and frame rate that match your project's shooting parameters. Common resolutions include 1080p (1920x1080) and 4K (3840x2160).

2. **Bitrate and Quality:** Adjust the bitrate to determine the quality and file size of the exported video. Higher bitrates generally result in better quality but larger file sizes.

3. **Codec Selection:** Choose a codec that suits your intended distribution. H.264 is widely supported and ideal for online streaming, while ProRes or DNxHR are suitable for high-quality production.

Understanding Different Video Formats: Navigating the Landscape:

1. **MP4:** A highly compressed format suitable for online streaming and sharing on social media platforms.

2. **MOV:** A versatile format used for high-quality videos and video editing. Commonly used for exporting intermediate or master files.

3. **AVI:** A legacy format suitable for Windows-based systems. Provides good quality but tends to result in larger file sizes.

Audio Export Settings: Harmonizing Soundscapes:

1. **Audio Codec:** Choose an audio codec that maintains the quality of your audio. AAC and MP3 are common choices for online distribution.

2. **Sample Rate and Bit Depth:** Use a sample rate of 48 kHz for video projects. A bit depth of 16-bit is sufficient for most scenarios, while 24-bit offers higher quality.

Exporting for Different Platforms: Tailoring Your Output:

1. **YouTube and Vimeo:** Utilize the built-in YouTube and Vimeo presets for seamless

uploads. These presets ensure that your video meets the platforms' requirements for optimal playback.

2. **Social Media Platforms:** Different platforms have varying requirements for video specifications. Adobe Premiere Pro offers presets for exporting videos optimized for platforms like Instagram, Facebook, and Twitter.

Previewing and Quality Control: The Final Checkpoint:
1. **Previewing Exported Videos:** Before sharing or publishing, review the exported video on various devices and screens to ensure that it looks and sounds as intended.

2. **Quality Control:** Check for artifacts, color shifts, or any issues that might have arisen during the export process. Make necessary adjustments and re-export if needed.

Conclusion: Transcending Vision through Export:
Understanding export settings and formats is the final step in the journey of video production, where your creative vision is transformed into a tangible product. With Adobe Premiere Pro's versatile export options, you have the power to customize your output for

different platforms, ensuring that your videos shine across a multitude of devices and screens. As you explore the intricacies of export settings, you're not just configuring parameters; you're optimizing your videos to be experienced exactly as you intended. By mastering the art of understanding export settings and formats, you ensure that your videos are not just seen and heard, but truly appreciated, across diverse audiences and platforms, transcending the boundaries of screens and leaving a lasting impression on viewers around the world.

Exporting for different platforms: web, social media, and broadcast

In the dynamic world of video production, sharing your content across different platforms requires careful consideration of technical specifications, formatting, and optimization. Adobe Premiere Pro, a realm of creative possibilities, offers a comprehensive toolkit for exporting videos tailored to specific platforms, ensuring that your content looks and sounds its best whether it's on the web, social media, or broadcast. In this comprehensive article, we'll delve into the art of exporting for different platforms, exploring techniques for optimizing video quality, meeting platform requirements, and captivating your audience across diverse digital landscapes.

The Multifaceted World of Exporting for Different Platforms: Crafting Tailored Experiences:
Exporting for different platforms involves translating your creative vision into formats that suit each platform's technical requirements and audience preferences. This ensures that your videos are well-received and perform optimally on various digital stages.

Export Settings and Format Selection: Platform-Specific Choices:
1. **Platform-Specific Presets:** Adobe Premiere Pro provides built-in presets that are optimized for various platforms, including YouTube, Vimeo, Instagram, Facebook, and more. These presets simplify the export process by aligning settings with platform requirements.

2. **Resolution and Aspect Ratio:** Different platforms have specific requirements for resolution and aspect ratio. Research the optimal settings for each platform to ensure your content displays correctly.

Exporting for the Web: Sharing on Websites and Online Platforms:
1. **Codec Choice:** For web distribution, the H.264 codec is widely recommended. It offers a

balance between video quality and file size, making it ideal for streaming.

2. **Bitrate and Quality:** Optimize the bitrate to maintain quality while minimizing file size. Lower bitrates are suitable for web streaming, where fast loading times are crucial.

3. **Frame Rate:** Use a frame rate of 30 or 60 frames per second (fps) for smooth playback. Higher frame rates are ideal for fast-paced content.

Exporting for Social Media Platforms: Engaging Audiences on Social Networks:

1. **Presets for Social Media:** Adobe Premiere Pro's presets for social media platforms like Instagram, Facebook, and Twitter ensure that your videos adhere to each platform's specifications.

2. **Video Duration:** Pay attention to video length restrictions on different platforms. For example, Instagram's Feed videos can be up to 60 seconds, while Stories are limited to 15 seconds.

3. **Aspect Ratio:** Social media platforms often have specific aspect ratio requirements. Common aspect ratios include 16:9

(landscape) and 9:16 (vertical) for Instagram Stories.

Exporting for Broadcast: Reaching Television Audiences:
1. **Broadcast Standards:** If your video is destined for television broadcast, adhere to the broadcast standards of your region. Different regions may have varying requirements for resolution, frame rate, and audio levels.

2. **Higher Bitrates:** Broadcast quality demands higher bitrates to ensure clear visuals on larger screens. Formats like ProRes or DNxHD are commonly used for high-quality broadcasts.

3. **Audio Levels:** Maintain consistent audio levels and ensure that dialogue and sound effects are clear and balanced, meeting the standards for broadcast audio.

Quality Control and Previewing: The Final Checks:
1. **Platform-Specific Playback:** Before publishing, review your exported videos on the intended platforms. Check for any formatting issues, aspect ratio discrepancies, or quality loss.

2. **Quality Control:** Carefully assess visual and audio quality to ensure that the exported

video retains its intended look and sound across different devices and screens.

Conclusion: Crafting Tailored Experiences Across Platforms:

Exporting for different platforms is an art that involves adapting your content to suit the preferences and technical requirements of each digital stage. With Adobe Premiere Pro's versatile export options, you have the power to create tailored experiences that captivate, engage, and resonate with audiences on the web, social media, and broadcast channels. As you navigate the complexities of exporting for various platforms, you're not just optimizing settings; you're crafting experiences that resonate with viewers, wherever they may be. By mastering the art of exporting for web, social media, and broadcast, you transcend the boundaries of screens, ensuring that your videos are not just seen and heard, but experienced in their full glory, leaving an indelible mark on audiences across diverse digital landscapes.

Creating custom export presets for future projects

In the realm of video production, efficiency and consistency are invaluable. The ability to recreate the optimal export settings for different projects can save time, streamline your workflow, and ensure consistent quality across your content. Adobe Premiere Pro, a hub of creative possibilities, offers the flexibility to create custom export presets that encapsulate your preferred settings. In this comprehensive article, we'll delve into the art of creating custom export presets, exploring techniques for saving time, maintaining quality, and fostering a seamless video production process across your future projects.

The Power of Custom Export Presets: Elevating Efficiency and Quality:
Custom export presets are the secret to consistency and efficiency in your video production process. They enable you to recreate specific export settings without the need to manually adjust parameters for every project.

Accessing Export Preset Options in Adobe Premiere Pro: Your Toolbox for Efficiency:
1. **Export Settings:** The Export Settings window in Adobe Premiere Pro is where you configure the various export parameters, including resolution, codec, bitrate, and more.

2. **Preset Creation:** Once you've customized the export settings to your liking, you can save them as a preset for future use. This ensures that you have a standardized template for similar projects.

Creating Custom Export Presets: Crafting Your Toolbox:

1. **Start with a Template:** Begin by configuring the export settings that align with your most common needs. This might include resolution, frame rate, codec, and bitrate.

2. **Save Preset:** Once you've fine-tuned the settings, navigate to the "Preset" dropdown menu in the Export Settings window and select "Save Preset." Give your preset a descriptive name for easy identification.

Fine-Tuning Your Export Presets: Adapting for Different Needs:

1. **Platform-Specific Presets:** Tailor export presets for specific platforms like YouTube, Vimeo, or social media. Adjust resolution, aspect ratio, and other settings to meet platform requirements.

2. **Quality and Bitrate Variations:** Create presets for different quality levels or bitrate requirements. This allows you to maintain consistent quality while accommodating various file size constraints.

3. **Audio Settings:** Custom export presets can include audio settings such as sample rate, bit

depth, and codec. Ensure that audio quality remains consistent across projects.

Recalling and Applying Custom Export Presets: Elevating Efficiency:

1. **Applying Presets:** When exporting a project, select your custom export preset from the "Preset" dropdown menu. This loads your predefined settings, saving you time and reducing the chance of errors.

2. **Editing Presets:** If your project's needs evolve, you can easily edit existing presets. Make adjustments to settings, update the preset, and save it with the same or a new name.

Quality Control and Previewing: Ensuring Consistency:

1. **Previewing Exported Videos:** Always review exported videos to ensure that they meet your intended quality standards. Playback on different devices to verify consistency.

2. **Fine-Tuning On-the-Fly:** Even with custom presets, each project may have unique requirements. Fine-tune settings within the preset to address specific project needs.

Conclusion: Unlocking Efficiency and Consistency:

Creating custom export presets is like building a toolbox of efficiencies that streamline your video production process. With Adobe Premiere Pro's custom export preset feature, you have the power to maintain consistent quality, adapt to various project needs, and save valuable time. As you explore the world of custom export presets, you're not just configuring settings; you're fostering a workflow that empowers creativity and elevates efficiency. By mastering the art of creating custom export presets, you transcend the routine and enter a realm where each project begins with a solid foundation, ensuring that your videos are not just creations, but meticulously crafted masterpieces that leave a lasting impression on your audience.

Sharing your work directly from Adobe Premiere Pro

In the realm of video production, the final step of sharing your masterpiece with the world should be as smooth as the creative journey itself. Adobe Premiere Pro, a realm of creative possibilities, offers an integrated sharing experience that allows you to seamlessly share your videos directly from the software. In this comprehensive article, we'll delve into the art of sharing your work from Adobe Premiere Pro, exploring techniques for exporting, publishing, and distributing your videos to various platforms, audiences, and screens.

The Power of Direct Sharing: Streamlining Your Workflow:

Direct sharing from Adobe Premiere Pro eliminates the need to exit the software and use separate tools for distribution. It streamlines your workflow, saves time, and ensures that your videos reach their intended audience with ease.

Accessing Sharing Options in Adobe Premiere Pro: Your Gateway to Distribution:

1. **Export Window:** The Export window in Adobe Premiere Pro serves as the hub for exporting and sharing your videos. Here, you'll find a range of options for customizing your output to meet your distribution needs.

2. **Social Media Integration:** Adobe Premiere Pro offers integration with various social media platforms, allowing you to share your videos directly to your accounts without leaving the software.

Sharing Techniques: Crafting Your Online Presence:

1. **Export Settings:** Choose the export settings that align with your distribution goals. Optimize resolution, bitrate, codec, and other parameters to ensure your video looks its best on different platforms.

2. **Platform-Specific Presets:** Adobe Premiere Pro provides presets tailored for various platforms, such as YouTube and Vimeo. These presets simplify the process by aligning settings with platform requirements.

3. **Social Media Integration:** When exporting, you can choose to directly share your video to platforms like YouTube, Vimeo, and Facebook. Authenticate your accounts, customize metadata, and publish seamlessly.

Sharing to Online Platforms: Reaching a Global Audience:

1. **YouTube:** Adobe Premiere Pro's direct sharing to YouTube allows you to upload videos with ease. Choose a preset, customize metadata, and publish your video to your channel directly from the software.

2. **Vimeo:** Whether for personal projects or professional portfolios, sharing to Vimeo is effortless. Add video details, set privacy options, and publish to your Vimeo account seamlessly.

Sharing on Social Media: Engaging Audiences on Digital Stages:

1. **Facebook:** Share your videos on Facebook directly from Adobe Premiere Pro. Customize your video's title, description, and thumbnail, and publish it to your profile or page.

2. **Twitter:** Sharing videos on Twitter becomes a breeze with Adobe Premiere Pro's integration. Add hashtags, captions, and a captivating thumbnail before sharing with your followers.

Quality Control and Review: The Final Checkpoint:

1. **Playback Verification:** Always review your shared videos on the intended platforms to ensure that they look and sound as intended. This ensures that your audience experiences the video as you intended.

2. **Engagement Monitoring:** Once your video is shared, monitor engagement metrics such as views, likes, comments, and shares. This provides insights into your video's reception and impact.

Conclusion: Empowering Distribution with Direct Sharing:

Sharing your work directly from Adobe Premiere Pro is the final flourish that transforms your creative endeavor into a shared experience. With Adobe Premiere Pro's integrated sharing options, you have the power to distribute your videos seamlessly to different platforms, audiences, and screens. As you navigate the world of direct sharing, you're not just sharing files; you're sharing stories, emotions, and narratives that resonate with viewers around the world. By mastering the art of sharing your work directly from Adobe Premiere Pro, you transcend the boundaries of screens, ensuring that your videos are not just seen and heard, but experienced, appreciated, and celebrated across diverse digital stages.

Chapter 8: Efficient Workflows and Productivity Tips
Keyboard shortcuts to speed up your editing process

In the fast-paced world of video editing, every second counts. The ability to execute commands swiftly and effortlessly can significantly impact your workflow, allowing you to focus on creativity rather than navigating menus. Adobe Premiere Pro, a realm of creative possibilities, offers a treasure trove of keyboard shortcuts that can revolutionize your editing process. In this comprehensive article, we'll delve into the art of using keyboard shortcuts to supercharge your editing, exploring techniques for improving efficiency, customizing shortcuts, and mastering the keyboard-driven dance that brings your visions to life.

The Power of Keyboard Shortcuts: Elevating Efficiency and Creativity:
Keyboard shortcuts are the secret weapons in a video editor's arsenal. They eliminate the need to manually navigate menus, empowering you to execute commands with a simple keystroke and enhancing your overall efficiency and productivity.

Accessing and Customizing Keyboard Shortcuts in Adobe Premiere Pro: Your Digital Palette:
1. **Keyboard Shortcuts:** Adobe Premiere Pro provides an extensive list of default keyboard shortcuts that cover a wide range of functions,

from basic tasks to advanced editing techniques.

2. **Keyboard Shortcuts Panel:** The Keyboard Shortcuts panel in Adobe Premiere Pro allows you to view, search, and customize shortcuts to suit your preferences and workflow.

Learning and Implementing Keyboard Shortcuts: Crafting Speed and Precision:

1. **Essential Shortcuts:** Start with the essential keyboard shortcuts that facilitate basic actions such as cutting, copying, pasting, and navigating the timeline.

2. **Navigation and Playhead Control:** Master shortcuts for moving the playhead, zooming in and out, and jumping between edit points. This streamlines your navigation through the timeline.

3. **Editing and Trimming:** Familiarize yourself with shortcuts for various editing tasks, such as ripple edits, rolling edits, and slip edits. These shortcuts optimize your precision when refining your sequences.

4. **Selection and Manipulation:** Learn shortcuts for selecting clips, moving them on the timeline, and adjusting their properties. This

allows you to manipulate elements with speed and ease.

5. **Effects and Transitions:** Shortcuts for applying and managing effects, transitions, and audio adjustments can significantly enhance your ability to shape the visual and auditory aspects of your project.

Customizing Keyboard Shortcuts: Tailoring Your Workflow:

1. **Keyboard Shortcuts Panel:** Use the Keyboard Shortcuts panel to customize existing shortcuts or create new ones that align with your editing habits and preferences.

2. **Shortcut Sets:** Adobe Premiere Pro offers predefined shortcut sets for different roles, such as editing, audio, and color correction. Customize these sets or create your own for specialized tasks.

Developing Muscle Memory and Workflow Efficiency:

1. **Practice:** Regularly use the keyboard shortcuts you've learned to reinforce your muscle memory. Over time, these shortcuts will become second nature.

2. **Efficiency Benefits:** The more keyboard shortcuts you integrate into your workflow, the faster you'll be able to perform tasks, leading to a more fluid and productive editing process.

Navigating the Timeline with Precision:
1. **J, K, and L Keys:** These keys allow you to shuttle forward (L) and backward (J) through the timeline, as well as pause (K) playback. Combining them with modifiers lets you navigate with precision.

2. **I and O Keys:** The I and O keys mark the in and out points on your timeline, facilitating efficient clip selection and trimming.

Conclusion: Elevating Your Craft with Keyboard Mastery:
Mastering keyboard shortcuts is like learning a dance that transforms your editing process. With Adobe Premiere Pro's vast array of keyboard shortcuts, you have the means to execute commands swiftly, navigate timelines with precision, and unleash your creative visions without interruption. As you explore the world of keyboard shortcuts, you're not just memorizing sequences of keys; you're honing your craft and creating a fluid, seamless, and efficient editing experience. By mastering the art of using keyboard shortcuts, you transcend the limitations of

mouse clicks and menus, harnessing the power of key combinations to elevate your storytelling, bring your visions to life, and craft videos that resonate with your audience on a profound level.

Creating and saving custom workspaces

In the realm of video editing, your workspace is your canvas—a place where creativity flourishes, ideas come to life, and stories unfold. Adobe Premiere Pro, a realm of creative possibilities, allows you to tailor your workspace to your unique needs, ensuring a seamless and efficient editing experience. In this comprehensive article, we'll delve into the art of creating and saving custom workspaces, exploring techniques for optimizing your layout, customizing panels, and curating a creative environment that elevates your video editing journey.

The Significance of Custom Workspaces: Fostering Productivity and Creativity:
Custom workspaces in Adobe Premiere Pro empower you to create a visual environment that enhances your productivity and creativity. By arranging panels, tools, and features according to your preferences, you can streamline your workflow and focus on what matters most—bringing your creative visions to life.

Accessing and Customizing Workspaces in Adobe Premiere Pro: Your Personal Studio:

1. **Workspaces Dropdown Menu:** Adobe Premiere Pro offers a range of default workspaces optimized for different tasks, such as editing, color grading, and audio mixing.

2. **Custom Workspace Creation:** Beyond the default options, you can create your own custom workspaces tailored to your specific needs, workflow, and editing style.

Creating Custom Workspaces: Crafting Your Ideal Canvas:

1. **Layout Optimization:** Start by organizing your panels in a way that maximizes your efficiency. Place frequently used panels where they're easily accessible, and group related panels together.

2. **Panel Arrangement:** Drag and dock panels to create a layout that suits your workflow. You can stack panels vertically or horizontally, resize them, and even float them for more flexibility.

3. **Removing Unused Panels:** If certain panels aren't essential to your workflow, you can remove them from your custom workspace to declutter your interface.

Customizing Panels and Toolbars: Tailoring Your Editing Toolkit:

1. **Panel Selection:** Choose the panels that align with your editing tasks. Adobe Premiere Pro offers a wide range of panels, from the Project panel to the Effects Controls panel.

2. **Toolbar Customization:** Customize the toolbar to include your most frequently used tools. By eliminating unnecessary tools, you can simplify your workspace and reduce visual clutter.

Saving Custom Workspaces: Preserving Your Creative Environment:

1. **Workspace Dropdown Menu:** Once you've arranged your panels and created a layout that suits your preferences, navigate to the Workspace dropdown menu and select "Save as New Workspace."

2. **Naming Your Workspace:** Give your custom workspace a descriptive name that reflects its purpose or your editing style. This makes it easy to identify and select later.

Reverting to Default Workspaces and Resetting Layouts:

1. **Resetting to Default:** If you ever wish to return to a default workspace, simply select the desired workspace from the dropdown menu. This resets the layout to its default configuration.

2. **Resetting Panels:** Adobe Premiere Pro also offers the option to reset specific panels to their default arrangement if you've made extensive changes.

Workflow Evolution and Adaptation:

1. **Evolving Needs:** As your projects and tasks change, your workspace needs may evolve. Don't hesitate to modify your custom workspace to accommodate new requirements.

2. **Adapting for Efficiency:** Regularly assess your workflow and adjust your custom workspace to reflect your most efficient processes. Customization ensures that your workspace remains a tailored and productive environment.

Conclusion: Forging Your Creative Sanctuary:

Creating and saving custom workspaces in Adobe Premiere Pro is like curating your own creative sanctuary—a place where your ideas flourish, your vision takes shape, and your editing process flows with efficiency. By mastering the art of custom workspaces, you're not just rearranging panels; you're designing an environment that inspires innovation and elevates your craft. By crafting your ideal canvas and harnessing the power of personalized workspaces, you transcend the limitations of default layouts, embracing an editing experience that is uniquely yours—one that empowers you to create videos that captivate, engage, and leave a lasting impression on your audience.

Utilizing markers and labels for organization

In the intricate realm of video editing, organization is the key to a streamlined and productive workflow. Adobe Premiere Pro, a realm of creative possibilities, equips you with a range of tools to keep your projects well-structured and your creative process flowing seamlessly. Among these tools, markers and labels stand out as powerful aids in maintaining clarity, navigating timelines, and enhancing collaboration. In this comprehensive article, we'll delve into the art of utilizing markers and labels to organize your projects, exploring techniques for annotating footage, synchronizing audio, adding context, and fostering a well-orchestrated editing experience.

The Essence of Markers and Labels: Elevating Organization and Collaboration:

Markers and labels are virtual signposts that guide you through the complexities of your project. By strategically placing markers and applying labels, you create a roadmap that enhances clarity, accelerates navigation, and facilitates effective collaboration with team members.

Accessing Markers and Labels in Adobe Premiere Pro: Your Organizational Toolbox:

1. **Markers Panel:** The Markers panel in Adobe Premiere Pro serves as the hub for creating and managing markers. Here, you can annotate clips, sequences, and points of interest within your project.

2. **Labeling Clips:** Labels, which can be assigned to clips, sequences, and more, provide visual cues that indicate the content, status, or importance of specific elements in your project.

Using Markers for Efficient Workflow:

1. **Types of Markers:** Adobe Premiere Pro offers several types of markers, including standard markers, chapter markers, and web links. Each type serves a distinct purpose in your project organization.

2. **In-Point and Out-Point Markers:** Place markers at the in and out points of clips to easily identify specific sections you want to work with. This speeds up the trimming and editing process.

3. **Scene Breaks and Transitions:** Markers can highlight scene breaks, transitions, or other significant moments in your footage, making it easier to locate and edit them.

Synchronizing Audio and Video with Markers:

1. **Audio Cue Points:** Place markers in sync with audio cues, such as beats or dialogue delivery. This ensures that your edits align perfectly with the rhythm and timing of the audio.

2. **Synchronizing Multi-Camera Footage:** When working with multi-camera footage, use markers to sync different angles by placing markers at the same visual or audio cues.

Labeling Clips for Context and Organization:

1. **Clip Status:** Assign labels to clips to indicate their status, such as "in progress," "review," or "finalized." This helps you and your team members keep track of the editing progress.

2. **Categorization:** Use labels to categorize clips based on content, location, characters, or any other relevant criteria. This makes it easier to locate specific clips later.

Collaboration and Project Communication:
1. **Adding Notes:** Attach notes to markers to provide context, instructions, or reminders for yourself and collaborators. Notes can convey details about specific edits, changes, or ideas.

2. **Exporting Markers:** When sharing your project with team members, you can export markers to ensure that everyone is on the same page regarding edit points, notes, and annotations.

Customizing Markers and Labels for Your Workflow:
1. **Label Colors:** Customize label colors to match your workflow preferences. Assign specific colors to different types of content or categories for easy visual identification.

2. **Marker Options:** Adobe Premiere Pro offers options to customize marker icons and durations. This allows you to differentiate markers based on their purpose or importance.

Conclusion: Guiding Your Creative Journey with Precision:

Utilizing markers and labels in Adobe Premiere Pro is like laying down a trail of breadcrumbs that guides you through the labyrinth of video editing. By mastering the art of using markers and labels, you're not just annotating footage; you're enhancing organization, optimizing navigation, and fostering effective collaboration. As you explore the world of markers and labels, you're not just creating virtual signposts; you're orchestrating a symphony of clarity, communication, and creativity. By harnessing the power of these organizational tools, you transcend the challenges of complexity and chaos, forging a path of precision and purpose that leads to videos that are not just edited, but meticulously curated expressions of your vision.

Collaboration techniques: sharing projects and working in teams

In the dynamic landscape of video production, collaboration is the heartbeat that propels projects from concepts to captivating realities. Adobe Premiere Pro, a realm of creative possibilities, is designed to facilitate seamless teamwork, enabling individuals to merge their talents, insights, and perspectives into a cohesive masterpiece. In this comprehensive article, we'll delve into the art of collaboration techniques in Adobe Premiere Pro, exploring strategies for sharing projects, managing version control, optimizing workflows, and embracing the power of collective creativity.

The Essence of Collaboration: Fostering Synergy and Creativity:
Collaboration is more than just a practical necessity—it's a catalyst for innovation. Adobe Premiere Pro empowers creators to come together, pooling their skills and visions to create videos that transcend individual efforts.

Accessing Collaboration Tools in Adobe Premiere Pro: Your Path to Collective Excellence:
1. **Project Sharing:** Adobe Premiere Pro offers robust tools for sharing projects and collaborating in real-time. These tools facilitate a synchronized workflow among team members, no matter where they are located.

2. **Version Control:** Version control tools help prevent confusion and ensure that each team member is working with the latest version of the project. This minimizes errors and maximizes efficiency.

Collaboration Techniques for Project Sharing:
1. **Shared Projects:** Adobe Premiere Pro's Shared Projects feature enables multiple editors to work on the same project simultaneously. It's

a dynamic approach to collaboration that fosters real-time feedback and seamless contribution.

2. **Team Projects:** Team Projects is a cloud-based collaboration solution that enables remote teamwork. It allows editors, assistants, and other contributors to work together on projects hosted in the cloud.

Optimizing Collaboration Workflows:
1. **Project Organization:** Establish a clear project structure with organized bins, folders, and naming conventions. This structure ensures that team members can locate assets quickly and maintain consistency.

2. **Roles and Responsibilities:** Clearly define the roles and responsibilities of each team member. This ensures that everyone knows their tasks and contributions, minimizing duplication of effort.

3. **Communication Channels:** Use communication tools such as chat, video calls, or project management platforms to facilitate ongoing communication among team members. Open dialogue promotes clarity and keeps everyone aligned.

Version Control and Project Backups:

1. **Auto-Save and Backups:** Adobe Premiere Pro's auto-save and backup features help protect your work from unexpected crashes or system failures. Regularly save your project and enable the auto-save function.

2. **Project Version Naming:** Develop a version naming convention that reflects the project's progress and date. This simplifies tracking changes and ensures that everyone is working with the correct version.

Collaboration Etiquette and Best Practices:

1. **Respect and Feedback:** Foster a culture of respect and constructive feedback. Collaborators should feel comfortable sharing ideas and offering suggestions for improvement.

2. **File Naming and Organization:** Consistency in file naming and organization is crucial for smooth collaboration. Use descriptive names, avoid special characters, and adhere to a shared structure.

3. **Documentation:** Document important decisions, changes, and feedback. This documentation serves as a reference point

and helps maintain a clear record of the project's evolution.

Conclusion: A Symphony of Collective Creativity:
Collaboration techniques in Adobe Premiere Pro transform video production into a symphony of collective creativity. By mastering the art of collaboration, you're not just sharing files and tasks; you're building bridges between minds, uniting diverse talents, and creating videos that are greater than the sum of their parts. As you navigate the world of collaboration in Adobe Premiere Pro, you're not just managing projects; you're orchestrating a harmonious convergence of ideas, skills, and aspirations. By embracing the power of teamwork, you transcend the boundaries of individual creativity, giving life to videos that resonate, captivate, and leave a lasting impression on audiences around the world.

Chapter 9: Troubleshooting and Common Challenges
Dealing with playback and rendering issues

In the realm of video editing, technical challenges can sometimes disrupt the seamless flow of creativity. Adobe Premiere Pro, a realm of creative possibilities, offers a comprehensive toolkit to address playback and rendering issues that may arise during the editing process. In this comprehensive article, we'll delve into the art of troubleshooting playback and rendering issues in Adobe Premiere Pro, exploring techniques for identifying common problems, optimizing performance, and ensuring that your creative journey remains unhindered by technical hurdles.

The Complexities of Playback and Rendering: Ensuring Smooth Editing:

Playback and rendering are critical components of the editing process. Ensuring smooth playback allows you to visualize your edits, transitions, and effects, while efficient rendering is essential for producing the final video with high-quality output.

Identifying Playback and Rendering Issues: Diagnosing the Problem:

1. **Playback Lag:** If your playback is stuttering, freezing, or experiencing lag, it may be due to issues with system performance, media files, or sequence settings.

2. **Rendering Errors:** Rendering issues can manifest as incomplete or distorted frames, unexpected glitches, or system crashes during the rendering process.

Optimizing Performance for Smooth Playback:
1. **Proxy Workflow:** Utilize proxy media to reduce the strain on your system during editing. Proxy files are lower-resolution versions of your footage, allowing for smoother playback.

2. **Optimized Media:** Adobe Premiere Pro provides the option to create optimized media files for smoother playback. This is especially useful for high-resolution footage.

3. **Preview Quality:** Adjust the playback quality to a lower setting when editing. This improves real-time performance while still allowing you to see the edits clearly.

Addressing Rendering Issues: Troubleshooting Techniques:
1. **Media Cache:** Clear the media cache to free up storage space and potentially resolve rendering issues caused by cached data conflicts.

2. **Effects and Plugins:** Disable or remove effects or plugins that might be causing rendering errors. Sometimes, certain effects can conflict with rendering processes.

3. **Unrendered Effects:** Ensure that all effects and transitions in your sequence are properly rendered before finalizing your video. Unrendered effects can lead to unexpected issues during rendering.

Sequence Settings and Output Formats: Matching Settings for Smooth Playback:
1. **Sequence Settings:** Misaligned sequence settings can lead to playback and rendering issues. Ensure that your sequence settings match your media's resolution, frame rate, and aspect ratio.

2. **Output Formats:** Choose appropriate output formats that align with the distribution platforms for your video. Different formats have varying rendering requirements and considerations.

Hardware and System Performance: Ensuring Efficient Workflow:

1. **Hardware Requirements:** Check if your computer meets the minimum system requirements for Adobe Premiere Pro. Inadequate hardware can lead to performance issues.

2. **Driver Updates:** Keep your graphics card drivers up to date. Outdated drivers can contribute to playback and rendering problems.

Exporting and Rendering Settings: Quality and Performance Balance:

1. **Render Settings:** Adjust render settings to balance quality and performance. Optimize for your intended output while considering the capabilities of your hardware.

2. **Preview Render:** Adobe Premiere Pro allows you to render specific portions of your timeline for smoother playback. This can be particularly useful for complex sequences.

Regular Backups and Project Management:

1. **Backup Projects:** Regularly save backups of your project to prevent data loss in case of unexpected crashes or issues.

2. **Project Management:** Keep your project organized with well-structured bins, folders, and naming conventions. This minimizes the risk of media link issues and errors.

Conclusion: Navigating Technical Waters with Confidence:

Dealing with playback and rendering issues in Adobe Premiere Pro is a skill that empowers you to navigate the technical complexities of video editing with confidence. By mastering the art of troubleshooting, you're not just addressing problems; you're ensuring a seamless and uninterrupted creative journey. As you explore the world of playback and rendering, you're not just fixing glitches; you're optimizing performance, enhancing quality, and safeguarding the integrity of your video projects. By harnessing the power of troubleshooting techniques, you transcend the limitations of technical challenges, paving the way for videos that are not just edited, but refined, polished, and presented with the utmost precision and excellence.

Fixing audio and video synchronization problems

In the realm of video editing, maintaining the perfect harmony between audio and video is essential for creating a seamless and immersive viewer experience. Yet, audio and video synchronization issues can sometimes disrupt this delicate balance.

Adobe Premiere Pro, a realm of creative possibilities, offers a range of tools and techniques to address and fix audio and video synchronization problems that may arise during the editing process. In this comprehensive article, we'll delve into the art of fixing audio and video synchronization problems in Adobe Premiere Pro, exploring strategies for identifying the causes of sync issues, using various correction methods, and ensuring that your creative vision remains perfectly aligned.

The Importance of Audio and Video Synchronization: Preserving Immersion and Impact:

Audio and video synchronization is more than just technical precision; it's the heartbeat that connects visuals and emotions. Maintaining sync ensures that the audience experiences the intended impact of scenes, dialogue, and music.

Identifying Audio and Video Synchronization Issues: Diagnosing the Problem:

1. **Lip Sync Issues:** Misaligned lip movement with spoken dialogue can occur due to incorrect frame rates, dropped frames, or other technical discrepancies.

2. **Delay or Advance:** Audio and video may fall out of sync, with audio either preceding or lagging behind the corresponding video.

Correcting Audio and Video Synchronization: Troubleshooting Techniques:

1. **Frame Rate Mismatch:** Ensure that your project's frame rate matches the original media's frame rate. A mismatch can lead to gradual drifts in synchronization.

2. **Frame Dropping:** Frame dropping can occur during playback if your system's performance is strained. Optimize your system to prevent dropped frames that affect sync.

3. **Variable Frame Rates (VFR):** Footage shot with variable frame rates can lead to synchronization problems. Convert VFR footage to a constant frame rate to resolve issues.

Using Audio and Video Editing Techniques: Bringing Harmony to the Timeline:

1. **Slip and Slide Editing:** Utilize slip and slide editing techniques to adjust the timing of clips while keeping their relative positions intact. This is useful for fine-tuning sync.

2. **Audio Delay:** Apply audio delay to adjust the timing of the audio track, aligning it with the corresponding video. This is particularly effective for resolving minor sync issues.

3. **Speed/Duration Adjustment:** Altering the speed or duration of a clip can help restore synchronization. However, be cautious as this can affect the overall pacing of your project.

Syncing Audio and Video Manually: A Precise Approach:
1. **Clapperboard or Clap Sync:** If you have a visual or auditory marker, such as a clapboard or clap sound, use it to manually align audio and video tracks in post-production.

2. **Visual and Audio Cues:** Look for distinct visual cues, such as mouth movements or gestures, to guide your adjustments. Aligning these cues can help achieve accurate sync.

Using Audio Waveforms for Precision: Visual Alignment:
1. **Waveform Analysis:** Utilize the audio waveform in Adobe Premiere Pro to identify peak points, transients, or significant sound events that can aid in aligning audio and video.

2. **Zooming In:** Zoom in on the waveform to make precise adjustments. Align audio peaks or beats with corresponding visual cues to achieve accurate synchronization.

Avoiding Common Mistakes: Best Practices for Preventing Sync Issues:

1. **Recording Settings:** Ensure that recording devices are set to the same frame rate and sample rate. Consistency in settings prevents sync issues at the source.

2. **Monitoring Playback:** Regularly preview your project to detect any subtle synchronization issues before they become more pronounced.

3. **Backup and Duplicate Tracks:** Create backup tracks of your audio and video clips before making adjustments. This preserves your original content in case adjustments introduce new issues.

Conclusion: Navigating Sync Challenges with Precision:

Fixing audio and video synchronization problems in Adobe Premiere Pro is a skill that allows you to navigate the intricacies of creative harmony. By mastering the art of synchronization correction, you're not just aligning audio and video; you're preserving the magic of scenes, dialogues, and emotions. As you explore the world of synchronization correction, you're not just troubleshooting; you're ensuring that your creative vision resonates with audiences as intended. By harnessing the power of correction techniques, you transcend the boundaries of technical challenges, ensuring that your videos are not just synchronized, but perfectly orchestrated expressions of your storytelling prowess.

Solving common export errors

In the realm of video production, the final step of exporting your masterpiece is a crucial one, as it transforms your creative vision into a shareable reality. Adobe Premiere Pro, a realm of creative possibilities, equips you with a comprehensive toolkit for exporting videos of exceptional quality. However, export errors can occasionally disrupt this final stride. In this comprehensive article, we'll delve into the art of solving common export errors in Adobe Premiere Pro, exploring techniques for identifying issues, troubleshooting errors, and ensuring that your creative efforts culminate in a successful export.

The Significance of Export: Delivering Your Creative Vision:

Exporting is the bridge that connects your creative endeavors to your audience. It's the moment when your video transitions from the editing timeline to the screens of your viewers, making it essential to ensure that this transition is smooth and flawless.

Identifying Common Export Errors: Unraveling the Challenge:

1. **Playback Issues:** Exported videos may exhibit playback problems such as stuttering, freezing, or visual glitches. These issues can arise due to various factors, including codec compatibility and export settings.

2. **Audio Sync Problems:** Audio and video may fall out of sync in the exported video, leading to noticeable discrepancies between spoken words and lip movements.

3. **Color and Quality Issues:** Exported videos may appear different in terms of color, brightness, or quality compared to the editing timeline. This can result from incorrect export settings or color management issues.

Solving Playback and Quality Issues: Troubleshooting Techniques:

1. **Codec and Format Selection:** Choose the appropriate codec and format for your intended output. Incorrect choices can lead to compatibility issues and playback errors.

2. **Bitrate Settings:** Adjust the bitrate settings to ensure optimal video quality and file size. Very high or very low bitrates can result in playback problems or excessive file sizes.

3. **Export Settings Validation:** Double-check all export settings, including frame rate, resolution, and aspect ratio, to ensure they match your project's settings.

Addressing Audio Sync Problems: Precision in Sync:
1. **Source Footage Check:** Ensure that the audio and video sources within your editing project are correctly synced before exporting. Exporting unsynced sources will result in continued sync issues.

2. **Frame Rate Consistency:** Verify that your project's frame rate matches the original footage's frame rate. Mismatched frame rates can lead to gradual audio drift.

Handling Color and Quality Discrepancies: Color Management Mastery:
1. **Color Management Settings:** Adobe Premiere Pro's color management settings should match your project's color space and intended output. This ensures consistent color representation.

2. **Export Presets:** Utilize Adobe Premiere Pro's export presets that are optimized for specific platforms. These presets include correct color

profiles and settings for different types of media.

Dealing with Format and Codec Compatibility:
1. **Codec Compatibility:** Choose codecs that are widely accepted and compatible with the target platform. Some codecs may not be supported by certain players or platforms.

2. **Frame Size and Aspect Ratio:** Confirm that your export frame size and aspect ratio align with the target platform's requirements. Misaligned sizes can lead to cropping or distortion.

Exporting with Advanced Techniques:
1. **Export Queue and Media Encoder:** Use Adobe Media Encoder to export your videos, as it provides more flexibility, control, and options for handling export settings.

2. **Export Test:** Before sharing your final video, perform a test export with a short portion of your project to verify that there are no unexpected errors or discrepancies.

Conclusion: Crafting a Seamless Export Journey:
Solving common export errors in Adobe Premiere Pro is a skill that ensures your creative journey culminates in a polished, shareable video. By mastering the art of troubleshooting export errors, you're not just fixing glitches; you're enhancing your understanding of codecs, formats, and settings. As you explore the world of export error resolution, you're not just addressing issues; you're refining your technical prowess, optimizing your workflow, and guaranteeing that your videos are presented to the world in the best possible form. By harnessing the power of error-solving techniques, you transcend the challenges of technical complexities, delivering videos that aren't just exported, but meticulously curated expressions of your creative brilliance.

Troubleshooting performance and system compatibility

In the dynamic world of video editing, the synergy between your creative vision and your editing tool is vital. Adobe Premiere Pro, a realm of creative possibilities, empowers you to shape your ideas into compelling visual narratives. However, issues related to performance and system compatibility can sometimes hinder the seamless realization of your creative dreams. In this comprehensive article, we'll delve into the art of troubleshooting performance and system compatibility issues in Adobe Premiere Pro, exploring techniques for identifying common problems, optimizing performance, and ensuring that your creative journey remains unhindered by technical obstacles.

The Essence of Performance and Compatibility: The Backbone of Creativity:

Performance and system compatibility form the foundation of your editing experience. Efficient performance ensures that your creative workflow remains fluid, while system compatibility guarantees that your hardware can handle the demands of video editing.

Identifying Performance and System Compatibility Issues: Diagnosing the Problem:

1. **Lag and Slowdowns:** If your workflow is marked by sluggish response, delayed playback, or unresponsive controls, performance issues may be at play.

2. **Crashes and Errors:** Frequent crashes, unexpected freezes, or error messages can indicate compatibility issues between Adobe Premiere Pro and your system.

Optimizing Performance for Efficient Editing:

1. **Hardware Requirements:** Verify that your computer meets the minimum system requirements for Adobe Premiere Pro.

Inadequate hardware can lead to performance problems.

2. **System Updates:** Regularly update your operating system and graphics card drivers to ensure compatibility with Adobe Premiere Pro's latest versions.

3. **Background Processes:** Close unnecessary background applications and processes that may consume system resources, diverting them from your editing software.

Maximizing Performance with Project Optimization:
1. **Proxy Workflow:** Utilize proxy media to reduce the strain on your system during editing. Proxy files are lower-resolution versions of your footage that allow for smoother playback.

2. **Optimized Media:** Adobe Premiere Pro provides the option to create optimized media files for improved playback performance, particularly when working with high-resolution footage.

3. **Preview Quality:** Adjust the playback quality to a lower setting during editing. This enhances real-time performance without

sacrificing your ability to assess edits accurately.

Addressing Crashes and Compatibility Errors: Troubleshooting Techniques:

1. **Plugin and Effect Compatibility:** Verify that third-party plugins and effects are compatible with your Adobe Premiere Pro version. Incompatible plugins can lead to crashes.

2. **Hardware Acceleration:** Experiment with hardware acceleration settings, such as GPU acceleration, to determine if they contribute to crashes or instability.

System Compatibility: A Holistic Approach:

1. **RAM and Storage:** Sufficient RAM and fast storage are essential for smooth editing. Insufficient memory or slow storage can lead to performance bottlenecks.

2. **Project Complexity:** Highly complex projects with numerous effects, layers, and high-resolution media can strain your system. Consider simplifying complex sequences to enhance performance.

Troubleshooting Common Performance Issues: Best Practices:

1. **Regular Backups:** Regularly save backup copies of your project to prevent data loss in case of crashes. Backups ensure you can resume work from a stable point.

2. **Project File Integrity:** Corrupted project files can lead to crashes and unexpected behavior. Use the "Project Manager" feature to collect and archive your project's media and sequences.

Conclusion: Mastering the Performance and Compatibility Balance:

Troubleshooting performance and system compatibility issues in Adobe Premiere Pro is a skill that empowers you to navigate the intricate terrain of video editing with confidence. By mastering the art of troubleshooting, you're not just addressing technical challenges; you're optimizing your workflow, enhancing your technical knowledge, and safeguarding the integrity of your creative process. As you delve into the world of performance and compatibility troubleshooting, you're not just fixing problems; you're refining your editing environment, fine-tuning your system, and ensuring that your videos are brought to life in a seamless and efficient manner. By harnessing the power of troubleshooting techniques, you transcend the boundaries of technical obstacles, crafting videos that aren't just edited, but expertly orchestrated expressions of your creative brilliance.

Chapter 10: Beyond the Basics: Advanced Techniques
Green screen (chroma key) editing

The magic of filmmaking often lies in the ability to transport audiences to different worlds and times, all within the confines of a screen. Green screen (chroma key) technology is a powerful tool that empowers creators to defy the limitations of physical locations, enabling them to merge live-action footage with virtual environments seamlessly. Adobe Premiere Pro, a realm of creative possibilities, offers a robust suite of tools for mastering green screen editing. In this comprehensive article, we'll delve into the art of green screen editing in Adobe Premiere Pro, exploring techniques for achieving flawless results, handling challenges, and transforming your creative visions into captivating visual realities.

The Essence of Green Screen Editing: Breathing Life into Imagination:
Green screen editing is the gateway to bringing the fantastical and the impossible to life. It's a technique that empowers creators to replace a solid-colored background (often green or blue) with a digitally crafted environment, creating the illusion of being anywhere in the world—or beyond.

Understanding the Green Screen Process: Key Steps to Success:

1. **Filming with a Green Screen:** The process begins with shooting your subject against a uniform green background. Green is chosen because it contrasts with most human skin tones, making it easier to extract and replace in post-production.

2. **Selecting Keying Software:** Adobe Premiere Pro offers powerful chroma keying tools that allow you to remove the green background and replace it with the desired background footage or image.

Achieving Flawless Green Screen Editing: Mastering the Techniques:

1. **Keying Techniques:** Adobe Premiere Pro provides several keying techniques, including Ultra Key and Keylight, which enable you to extract the green color accurately while retaining the subject's details.

2. **Refining Matte:** Adjust the keying settings to fine-tune the matte around the subject. This minimizes color spill and ensures a clean separation between the subject and the background.

Handling Common Challenges: Dealing with Spill and Transparency:

1. **Color Spill:** Sometimes, green or blue light from the screen can spill onto the subject, resulting in a colored tint. Use the spill suppression tools in Adobe Premiere Pro to correct this issue.

2. **Transparency Issues:** Ensure that the subject's edges remain crisp and detailed by addressing transparency issues caused by uneven lighting or motion blur.

Matching Lighting and Perspective: Adding Realism to the Scene:

1. **Lighting Consistency:** Match the lighting of the subject to that of the background to ensure a natural blend. Use Adobe Premiere Pro's color correction tools to adjust brightness, contrast, and color balance.

2. **Perspective and Depth:** Pay attention to the subject's placement in the scene, considering perspective and depth to create a convincing interaction between the subject and the virtual environment.

Creating Seamless Interactions: Compositing Realism and Believability:

1. **Interaction Elements:** To make the subject appear convincingly integrated into the new environment, consider adding shadows, reflections, and depth of field effects using Adobe Premiere Pro's visual effects tools.

2. **Matching Grain and Texture:** Apply grain and texture adjustments to the subject to ensure that it matches the background's visual characteristics, enhancing overall realism.

Utilizing Advanced Tools: Exploring Keying Adjustments and Tracking:

1. **Fine-Tuning Edges:** Adobe Premiere Pro offers tools for refining the edges of your subject to make them blend seamlessly with the new background.

2. **Motion Tracking:** When your subject moves within the frame, use motion tracking to ensure that the replacement background follows the subject's movements accurately.

Optimizing Workflow: Best Practices for Efficiency:

1. **Well-Lit Set:** Proper lighting is crucial for achieving clean keying. Use even, diffused lighting to minimize shadows and color inconsistencies.

2. **High-Quality Footage:** Shoot in the highest resolution possible to preserve detail during the keying process.

3. **Neutral Colors:** Avoid wardrobe and props that match the green or blue screen color, as these can lead to color spill and keying challenges.

Conclusion: Crafting Visual Wonders with Green Screen Mastery:

Green screen editing in Adobe Premiere Pro is a skill that empowers you to transcend physical limitations and create captivating visual narratives. By mastering the art of green screen editing, you're not just removing backgrounds; you're transforming imagination into reality. As you explore the world of green screen techniques, you're not just editing footage; you're merging reality and fantasy, crafting scenes that captivate and mesmerize. By harnessing the power of green screen tools, you transcend the boundaries of ordinary filmmaking, paving the way for videos that aren't just edited, but ingeniously crafted expressions of your boundless creativity.

Time remapping and speed manipulation

Time, a fundamental dimension of storytelling, holds the power to shape narratives, evoke emotions, and alter perspectives. Adobe Premiere Pro, a realm of creative possibilities, empowers editors to wield time as a malleable tool through time remapping and speed manipulation. In this comprehensive article, we'll delve into the art of time remapping and speed manipulation in Adobe Premiere Pro, exploring techniques for controlling time dynamics, achieving dramatic effects, and transforming your videos into captivating visual journeys.

The Essence of Time Remapping and Speed Manipulation: Embracing Creative Temporal Control:
Time remapping and speed manipulation are creative techniques that allow editors to manipulate the speed of clips, sequences, and footage, enabling them to accentuate moments, convey emotions, and orchestrate pacing.

Understanding Time Remapping: Manipulating Time Dynamics:
1. **Basic Speed Adjustment:** Adobe Premiere Pro allows you to change the speed of a clip or sequence, altering its duration and pace while maintaining its visual and auditory components.

2. **Time Stretching and Compression:** Time stretching lengthens or shortens clips, preserving their frame-to-frame relationship. Compression speeds up or slows down a clip without altering its playback duration.

Achieving Dramatic Effects: Slow Motion and Fast Motion Mastery:
1. **Slow Motion:** Slowing down footage imparts a sense of weight, emphasis, and immersion. It's ideal for capturing details, emphasizing emotions, and enhancing visual impact.

2. **Fast Motion:** Speeding up footage creates a sense of urgency, dynamic movement, and rapid progression. It's effective for compressing time or conveying energetic sequences.

Creating Seamless Time Transitions: Crossfades and Time Ramping:
1. **Crossfades:** Use crossfades to transition between normal speed and altered speed footage smoothly. Crossfades prevent jarring visual shifts and maintain viewer engagement.

2. **Time Ramping:** Gradually change the speed of a clip using time ramping. This technique ensures smooth speed transitions, whether for dramatic buildups or gradual decelerations.

Advanced Techniques: Time Remapping Beyond Speed:

1. **Speed Ramps and Variable Speeds:** Create dynamic effects by applying speed ramps, where the speed changes gradually within a specified time range.

2. **Freeze Frames and Time Effects:** Insert freeze frames to pause action at a specific moment, emphasizing details or allowing for narrative reflection.

Mastering Audio Effects with Speed Manipulation: Sound Dynamics:

1. **Maintaining Pitch:** Adobe Premiere Pro's Preserve Pitch feature ensures that audio maintains its natural pitch while the speed is adjusted.

2. **Pitch Shift:** Experiment with pitch shift effects to match audio to altered speeds, enhancing synchronization and auditory consistency.

Optimizing Workflow: Best Practices for Precision:

1. **Frame Rate Consistency:** Keep frame rates consistent to avoid synchronization issues when adjusting speed or time.

2. **Cut on Motion:** When changing speed within a clip, cut on motion to hide abrupt changes and ensure a smoother visual transition.

Utilizing Keyframes for Creative Control: Visual and Temporal Dynamics:

1. **Keyframe Animation:** Apply keyframes to control the speed and time dynamics of clips over time, allowing for intricate speed variations and seamless transitions.

2. **Temporal Effects:** Combine time remapping with other effects, such as color grading or motion blur, to achieve comprehensive visual transformations.

Conclusion: Crafting Time as a Creative Medium:

Time remapping and speed manipulation in Adobe Premiere Pro is a skill that empowers you to shape narratives, evoke emotions, and orchestrate visual symphonies. By mastering the art of temporal control, you're not just altering speed; you're molding time to amplify storytelling. As you delve into the world of time dynamics, you're not just editing footage; you're curating experiences, enhancing sequences, and engaging viewers on a deeper temporal level. By harnessing the power of time manipulation, you transcend the limitations of linear storytelling, crafting videos that aren't just edited, but meticulously sculpted expressions of your mastery over time's artistic canvas.

Advanced color grading and correction

Color, an evocative language in its own right, has the power to shape emotions, moods, and storytelling nuances. Adobe Premiere Pro, a realm of creative possibilities, provides a rich palette of tools for advanced color grading and correction, allowing editors to transform their videos from raw captures to captivating visual narratives. In this comprehensive article, we'll delve into the art of advanced color grading and correction in Adobe Premiere Pro, exploring techniques for enhancing aesthetics, conveying emotions, and transforming your videos into mesmerizing works of visual art.

The Essence of Advanced Color Grading and Correction: Elevating Visual Impact:
Advanced color grading and correction go beyond mere color adjustment; they're the art of elevating visuals to a higher level of aesthetics and storytelling impact. It's the mastery of light, color, and contrast to evoke emotions and immerse viewers in your narrative.

Understanding Color Grading and Correction: Layers of Color Mastery:
1. **Color Correction:** This involves adjusting the primary elements of color—red, green, and

blue—to correct color imbalances, ensuring accurate representation of scenes.

2. **Color Grading:** Grading is the creative process of altering the visual tone of a video to convey specific moods, aesthetics, and storytelling nuances.

Enhancing Visual Aesthetics: Achieving Cinematic Brilliance:
1. **Color Wheels and Curves:** Utilize color wheels and curves to finely adjust color balance and contrast, enhancing visual depth and richness.

2. **LUTs (Look-Up Tables):** Apply LUTs to instantly apply pre-designed color grades, achieving cinematic looks that emulate specific film styles.

Conveying Emotions with Color: Evoking Storytelling Nuances:
1. **Cool and Warm Tones:** Employ cool tones for melancholic or reflective scenes, and warm tones for creating a sense of intimacy or comfort.

2. **High and Low Contrast:** Adjust contrast levels to evoke different emotions—high contrast

for dynamic scenes and low contrast for softer, dreamy visuals.

Creating Consistency: Matching Scenes and Sequences:
1. **Shot Matching:** Ensure color consistency across shots and sequences to maintain visual coherence, even when scenes were shot under varying lighting conditions.

2. **Secondary Color Correction:** Isolate specific color ranges—such as skin tones—and adjust them independently for precise enhancements or corrections.

Managing Skin Tones: Achieving Natural Beauty:
1. **Skin Tone Adjustments:** Utilize color wheels to fine-tune skin tones, achieving natural and flattering appearances.

2. **HSL (Hue, Saturation, Lightness) Adjustments:** Modify specific color ranges—like the reds and oranges of skin tones—to achieve accurate and appealing results.

Utilizing Scopes for Precision: Data-Driven Color Mastery:

1. **Waveform Monitor:** Use the waveform monitor to analyze luminance levels and ensure proper exposure and contrast.

2. **Vectorscope:** The vectorscope helps maintain accurate color levels and balance, preventing color casts or imbalances.

Applying Grading Styles and Techniques: Crafting Visual Poetry:

1. **Vintage Looks:** Apply grading styles that emulate vintage film aesthetics, adding nostalgia and depth to your visuals.

2. **Day to Night Transitions:** Transform day scenes into night shots by adjusting color balance, contrast, and tones to evoke different lighting conditions.

Advanced Techniques: Exploring Color Effects and Fusion:

1. **Power Windows:** Apply selective color grading to specific areas of the frame, such as adjusting the exposure of a subject's face while maintaining the background.

2. **Fusion with Effects:** Combine color grading with other visual effects, like motion graphics or vignettes, to craft comprehensive visual experiences.

Optimizing Workflow: Best Practices for Brilliance:
1. **Reference Images:** Use reference images from your desired mood or style to guide your color grading decisions.

2. **Backup Projects:** Save versions of your color-graded project to preserve different grading stages and experiment with multiple looks.

Conclusion: Crafting Visual Symphony with Color Mastery:
Advanced color grading and correction in Adobe Premiere Pro is a skill that empowers you to orchestrate emotions, aesthetics, and storytelling nuances through the language of color. By mastering the art of advanced color manipulation, you're not just altering hues; you're imbuing scenes with emotions and atmospheres. As you explore the world of color grading and correction, you're not just editing visuals; you're painting visual stories, evoking sentiments, and guiding audiences through meticulously crafted sensory journeys. By harnessing the power of color, you transcend the boundaries of ordinary editing, creating videos that aren't just

edited, but intricately woven tapestries of your mastery over visual expression.

Creating visual effects using Adobe Premiere Pro
Visual effects (VFX) are the magic that transforms ordinary footage into extraordinary visual spectacles, adding layers of depth, excitement, and imagination to videos. Adobe Premiere Pro, a realm of creative possibilities, offers a plethora of tools and techniques for creating stunning visual effects that captivate and engage audiences. In this comprehensive article, we'll delve into the art of creating visual effects using Adobe Premiere Pro, exploring techniques for enhancing scenes, adding cinematic flair, and turning your videos into captivating visual journeys.

The Essence of Visual Effects: Transforming Realities into Fantasies:
Visual effects are the gateway to bringing imagination to life. Whether it's adding fantastical elements, altering environments, or creating jaw-dropping action sequences, VFX empower creators to push the boundaries of visual storytelling.

Understanding Visual Effects Creation: Layers of Digital Mastery:
1. **Compositing:** Compositing involves layering multiple elements—such as actors, backgrounds, and special effects—to create seamless and realistic visual compositions.

2. **Particle Effects:** Particle effects generate dynamic elements like fire, smoke, and explosions, adding realism and excitement to scenes.

Enhancing Scenes with Digital Magic: Adding Flair and Style:

1. **Color Grading and Correction:** Use color grading to transform the mood and tone of scenes, evoking emotions and creating visual coherence.

2. **Vignettes and Lighting Effects:** Add vignettes and lighting effects to draw attention to specific areas, create atmosphere, and enhance visual impact.

Creating Cinematic Flair: Elevating Dramatic Moments:

1. **Motion Graphics:** Integrate motion graphics elements like text, logos, or animations to convey information, enhance storytelling, and add style.

2. **Transitions and Warp Stabilization:** Apply dynamic transitions and stabilize shaky footage for seamless and professional-looking sequences.

Simulating Realism with Visual Effects: Crafting Authenticity:

1. **Green Screen (Chroma Key) Effects:** Replace green or blue screen backgrounds with alternate environments, seamlessly integrating actors and backgrounds.

2. **Virtual Set Extensions:** Create expansive and realistic environments by extending physical sets digitally, enhancing the visual scope of your scenes.

Applying Advanced Techniques: Fusion and Keyframing:

1. **Fusion with Effects:** Combine multiple effects to achieve complex visual results, such as adding motion graphics within composited scenes.

2. **Keyframing:** Utilize keyframes to animate properties of effects over time, creating dynamic transformations and evoking movement.

Crafting Dynamic Sequences: Explosions, Fire, and More:

1. **Particle Emitters:** Add particle emitters to create effects like rain, snow, or sparks, enhancing visual depth and realism.

2. **Explosions and Fire:** Incorporate explosion and fire effects to simulate action-packed scenes, adding excitement and drama.

Optimizing Workflow: Best Practices for Artistry:
1. **Pre-Visualization:** Plan your visual effects in advance with storyboards or animatics to ensure a clear vision before diving into editing.

2. **Footage Organization:** Label and organize your footage to easily locate and manipulate the elements you need for your visual effects.

Utilizing Expressions and Tracking: Precision in Digital Mastery:
1. **Expressions:** Employ expressions to automate animation and effect adjustments, enhancing efficiency and precision.

2. **Motion Tracking:** Use motion tracking to match effects to moving objects or characters, ensuring realistic integration within scenes.

Conclusion: Forging Visual Wonders with Adobe Premiere Pro:
Creating visual effects using Adobe Premiere Pro is a skill that empowers you to transform videos into captivating visual journeys. By mastering the art of

visual effects creation, you're not just manipulating pixels; you're crafting digital symphonies that captivate and mesmerize. As you explore the world of VFX, you're not just editing footage; you're adding layers of depth, style, and magic to scenes, breathing life into your creative visions. By harnessing the power of visual effects tools, you transcend the boundaries of reality, creating videos that aren't just edited, but masterfully orchestrated expressions of your digital artistry.

Conclusion
Reflecting on your journey from novice to Adobe Premiere Pro enthusiast

The path of a creative journey is often marked by twists, turns, and transformations that lead to growth, mastery, and a deep connection with one's chosen craft. As a novice setting foot on the shores of Adobe Premiere Pro, the journey to becoming an enthusiast is a profound tale of exploration, challenges, triumphs, and the gradual unfolding of creative potential. In this reflective article, we'll delve into the personal narrative of transitioning from a novice to an Adobe Premiere Pro enthusiast, exploring the lessons learned, milestones achieved, and the boundless passion ignited along the way.

The Novice's Prelude: The Exploration Begins:
Every journey begins with curiosity, and my journey with Adobe Premiere Pro was no exception. As a novice, the interface felt like an uncharted territory, a

canvas waiting to be painted with the strokes of creative expression. With its panels, timelines, and intricate toolset, Adobe Premiere Pro was a realm of endless possibilities, eagerly inviting me to explore its depths.

Navigating the Learning Curve: Challenges and Insights:
The initial steps were marked by challenges, as any novice's journey would be. The array of tools, effects, and settings presented a formidable learning curve. Yet, within each challenge, there lay an invaluable lesson. I discovered the importance of patience, persistence, and the willingness to seek knowledge. Tutorials, guides, and online communities became my allies, guiding me through the maze of techniques, shortcuts, and terminology.

The Spark of Achievement: Milestones Along the Way:
With every milestone reached, the enthusiasm grew. The first seamless edit, the realization of a visual effect, and the creation of a harmonious color grade— all became markers of progress. These milestones weren't just technical accomplishments; they were moments of triumph over self-doubt and uncertainty. Each achievement reaffirmed the belief that this journey was worth pursuing with unwavering dedication.

The Eureka Moments: Discovering Creative Expression:

Amidst the technical challenges, the true magic of Adobe Premiere Pro began to reveal itself—the ability to translate ideas into visual stories. The "aha" moments came when I realized that every tool, every effect, and every adjustment was a brushstroke on the canvas of my imagination. Color grading allowed me to evoke emotions, motion graphics enabled me to enhance storytelling, and time manipulation empowered me to shape narratives with temporal finesse. These were the moments when I discovered the true essence of creative empowerment.

Embracing the Editing Rhythm: Flow and Intuition:

As proficiency grew, so did the rhythm of editing. The constant toggling between panels became seamless, and the keyboard shortcuts became second nature. What was once a mechanical process evolved into an intuitive dance—a dance between footage and ideas, between visual effects and storytelling. The gaps between novice and enthusiast were bridged by countless hours spent in the editing suite, refining the craft and internalizing the intricacies of Adobe Premiere Pro.

Igniting the Flame of Enthusiasm: A Passion Unveiled:

The journey from novice to Adobe Premiere Pro enthusiast was not just about mastering a tool; it was about igniting a passion. The enthusiasm that had once been sparked by curiosity now burned brighter, fueled by the endless possibilities that this editing software presented. It was the thrill of experimenting with new effects, the joy of witnessing a video come to life, and the satisfaction of sharing a creative vision with the world.

The Journey Continues: Evolving Creatively:

As an Adobe Premiere Pro enthusiast, the journey doesn't end—it evolves. The skills, techniques, and insights gained continue to shape the creative process. Each project becomes an opportunity to push boundaries, experiment with new approaches, and create videos that resonate deeply with audiences. The journey, once marked by challenges, has transformed into a fluid dance of artistic expression.

In Conclusion: A Journey Woven with Passion:

The journey from novice to Adobe Premiere Pro enthusiast is a testament to the power of passion, persistence, and creative exploration. It's a journey marked by challenges that morph into triumphs, and a path that transforms technical skills into artistic mastery. The novice's exploration evolves into the enthusiast's artistic odyssey—an odyssey where the canvas of Adobe Premiere Pro becomes a tapestry woven with the threads of creativity, dedication, and the boundless joy of creating.

Embracing a continuous learning mindset for ongoing improvement

In the dynamic world of creative endeavors, the quest for improvement is a journey that never truly ends. Whether you're a novice stepping into the realm of Adobe Premiere Pro or an experienced enthusiast, the concept of continuous learning is the driving force that propels you toward greater heights of mastery and creativity. In this comprehensive article, we'll delve into the art of embracing a continuous learning mindset for ongoing improvement in Adobe Premiere Pro, exploring the benefits, strategies, and the transformative impact of never ceasing to evolve.

The Power of Continuous Learning: Fueling Growth and Innovation:

Continuous learning is a philosophy that acknowledges the ever-changing landscape of creative tools and techniques. It's the recognition that standing still equates to stagnation, while embracing new knowledge and skills paves the way for innovation, creativity, and the evolution of your craft.

Benefits of a Continuous Learning Mindset: Elevating Your Journey:

1. **Adapting to Change:** Creative tools, software updates, and industry trends evolve. A continuous learning mindset allows you to adapt to these changes seamlessly.

2. **Unlocking New Horizons:** Learning brings new possibilities to light. Acquiring new skills or techniques can open doors to creative avenues you never considered before.

3. **Staying Relevant:** In a rapidly evolving field, staying up-to-date is essential for remaining relevant in the eyes of your audience and peers.

4. **Enhancing Efficiency:** Learning shortcuts, techniques, and workflow optimizations boosts your efficiency, allowing you to spend more time on the creative aspects of your work.

5. **Fueling Passion:** Learning keeps your passion alive. The thrill of discovery and the joy of mastering new skills breathe new life into your creative pursuits.

Strategies for Embracing Continuous Learning: Navigating the Path:
1. **Set Learning Goals:** Define specific skills, techniques, or areas you want to improve. Having clear goals directs your learning efforts toward tangible outcomes.

2. **Dedicate Time:** Allocate regular time for learning. Whether it's a few minutes each day

or dedicated sessions each week, consistent effort compounds over time.

3. **Curate Learning Resources:** Leverage online tutorials, courses, books, and forums to access a wealth of knowledge from seasoned professionals and experts.

4. **Experiment and Apply:** Apply what you learn. Experiment with new techniques, effects, and tools in Adobe Premiere Pro to solidify your understanding.

5. **Challenge Yourself:** Push your boundaries by taking on projects that require you to stretch your skills. Overcoming challenges accelerates growth.

6. **Learn from Mistakes:** Mistakes are stepping stones to improvement. Analyze your failures, identify areas for improvement, and apply what you've learned.

Leveraging Adobe Premiere Pro's Resources: Your Learning Arsenal:
1. **Official Tutorials:** Adobe offers a wealth of tutorials, guides, and resources tailored to Adobe Premiere Pro users. These materials cover various techniques, effects, and features.

2. **Online Communities:** Participate in online forums and communities dedicated to Adobe Premiere Pro. Engage in discussions, seek advice, and share your own insights.

3. **Courses and Workshops:** Explore both free and paid courses that delve into specific aspects of Adobe Premiere Pro. These courses often provide structured learning paths.

4. **Experimentation:** Adobe Premiere Pro's intuitive interface encourages experimentation. Play around with effects, tools, and settings to understand their impact.

The Transformative Impact: Evolving as a Creator:
Embracing a continuous learning mindset isn't just about acquiring technical skills; it's about evolving as a creator. Each nugget of knowledge gained, each new technique mastered, and each skill honed contributes to your creative identity. It's the cumulative effect of these efforts that transforms you from a passive user into an active creator, capable of weaving narratives, evoking emotions, and leaving an indelible mark on your audience.

In Conclusion: A Journey of Endless Discovery:
Embracing a continuous learning mindset in Adobe Premiere Pro is a journey that reshapes not only your technical skills but also your creative outlook. It's a

journey marked by curiosity, exploration, and the unending pursuit of improvement. As you embrace this mindset, you embark on a path of ongoing growth, where every new skill learned becomes a brushstroke in the canvas of your creative evolution. With Adobe Premiere Pro as your playground, and a relentless hunger for learning as your guiding star, you transcend the boundaries of what you once thought possible, becoming a perpetual source of inspiration and innovation in the world of visual storytelling.

Encouragement to explore more advanced video editing topics and techniques

In the realm of video editing, there exists a world beyond the basics—a vast and exhilarating terrain that beckons creative adventurers to explore its depths. While mastering the essentials of video editing is essential, delving into more advanced topics and techniques opens up a universe of creative possibilities that can elevate your work to new heights. In this inspiring article, we'll delve into the realm of advanced video editing, encouraging you to step boldly into uncharted territories, embrace new challenges, and transform your editing skills into a masterful craft.

Beyond the Basics: The Allure of Advanced Techniques:
While foundational video editing skills lay the groundwork, advanced techniques are the keystones

of innovation. They allow you to manipulate time, evoke emotions, and create visual wonders that captivate audiences. By embracing more advanced topics, you're not just editing videos; you're crafting cinematic narratives that resonate deeply.

The Thrill of Exploration: Fueling Creativity:
The journey into advanced video editing is not just about learning new tools—it's about igniting your creativity. It's the thrill of experimenting with visual effects, pushing the boundaries of storytelling, and crafting videos that leave lasting impressions. The more you explore, the more you'll discover your unique style and creative voice.

A World of Advanced Topics: Embrace the Challenge:
1. **Color Grading Mastery:** Dive deep into the art of color correction and grading. Learn to use color to evoke emotions, enhance storytelling, and achieve cinematic brilliance.

2. **Advanced Transitions:** Move beyond simple cuts and fades. Master intricate transitions like whip pans, match cuts, and intricate motion graphics-driven transitions.

3. **Visual Effects and Compositing:** Discover the magic of visual effects. Learn to composite elements seamlessly, create explosions, simulate environments, and add digital magic to your scenes.

4. **Advanced Motion Graphics:** Elevate your projects with intricate motion graphics. Craft animated titles, dynamic lower thirds, and visually striking graphic overlays.

5. **Multi-Camera Editing:** Explore the techniques of multi-camera editing for complex projects. Sync and edit footage from different angles to create dynamic and engaging videos.

Mastering Sound Design: Sound is half the experience. Learn to manipulate audio, apply advanced sound effects, and create immersive soundscapes that enhance your storytelling.

Crafting Story Arcs: Move beyond linear narratives. Learn to structure your videos with intricate story arcs, pacing, and character development, transcending traditional storytelling.

Embracing Fusion and Fusion Techniques: Fuse video editing with visual effects. Create complex compositions, integrate CGI elements, and achieve cinematic realism.

Workflow Optimization: Streamline your process by mastering keyboard shortcuts, presets, and automation techniques. Efficient workflows free up more time for creative experimentation.

Expanding Your Creative Arsenal: Resources for Advancement:

1. **Online Courses and Tutorials:** The internet is a treasure trove of knowledge. Enroll in advanced video editing courses, or watch tutorials from experts in the field.

2. **Professional Communities:** Join online communities, forums, and social media groups dedicated to advanced video editing. Engage in discussions, seek advice, and share your discoveries.

3. **Collaboration and Critique:** Collaborate with fellow editors, exchange ideas, and seek constructive criticism. Learning from others accelerates growth.

4. **Industry Events and Workshops:** Attend workshops, seminars, and industry events to learn from professionals, expand your network, and immerse yourself in the latest trends.

In Conclusion: Your Odyssey Awaits:

Embracing advanced video editing topics and techniques is not just an evolution of your skills; it's an odyssey of creative exploration. It's a journey where you harness the tools, techniques, and knowledge to turn your videos into cinematic masterpieces. As you venture into the realm of advanced editing, you're not just a video editor; you're an artist, a storyteller, and a creator of visual wonders. So, heed the call to adventure, set sail into the unknown, and let your passion for advanced video editing shape your destiny as a masterful visual storyteller.

www.ingramcontent.com/pod-product-compliance
Lightning Source LLC
LaVergne TN
LVHW051331050326
832903LV00031B/3473